SOME OF MY RELIGION

BY THE
SAME AUTHOR

SHEPPARD'S PIE
(An Anthology)

Some of My Religion

by

H. R. L. SHEPPARD, C.H., D.D.

CASSELL & CO. LTD.

LONDON, TORONTO, MELBOURNE
AND SYDNEY

First Published 1935

PRINTED IN GREAT BRITAIN BY EBENEZER
BAYLIS AND SON, LIMITED, THE TRINITY
PRESS, WORCESTER, AND LONDON

F75.735

SOME OF MY RELIGION

O Brother man! fold to thy heart thy brother;
Where pity dwells, the peace of God is there;
To worship rightly is to love each other,
Each smile a hymn, each kindly deed a prayer.

Follow with reverent steps the great example
Of Him whose holy work was 'doing good';
So shall the wide earth seem our Father's temple,
Each loving life a psalm of gratitude.

Then shall all shackles fall; the stormy clangour
Of wild war music o'er the earth shall cease;
Love shall tread out the baleful fire of anger,
And in its ashes plant the tree of peace!

J. G. WHITTIER.

PREFACE

I AM certain that nothing is more native to man than religion; I am clear also that he is totally uninterested in most of the problems that agitate the Churches. Here I think he is right, for undoubtedly a considerable number of them have nothing to do with the religion of Jesus Christ, and some have nothing to do with religion at all. Yet man remains incurably religious and Jesus remains to him the last word in wisdom. We do not find fault with our neighbour because he is like Him, but because he is so unlike Him.

The average man, with all his faults, is ready for a surprising amount of Christianity if only its leaders would show him the vital heart of the Gospel. There must needs be a Christian Society, even though the genius of Christianity does not seem at home in our Church and Chapel atmosphere, since group organization is still essential for mankind.

Men and women are not often religiously or socially at their best in isolation. But if this Society is to be true to its Founder, and of service to humanity, it really must begin to realize that the Church was made for man, and not man for the Church. The clergy must come right down from their pedestals of aloofness and archaic reflections and meet men and women where they actually are, so that they may hear in their own tongue the wonderful works of God. Believe me, this need not entail nor permit "cheapening the Gospel," that Jones may be invited to accept only so much as he is willing to receive.

I am well aware that no great cause can for long hold the allegiance of the virile if, in an amiable desire to make converts, it covers over or makes light of its essential notes of urgency and sternness; and yet I resent, with all my soul, the fact that to-day the orthodox have so complicated the perfectly straightforward teaching of Christ that the "common people" neither hear Him gladly nor with understanding. Christianity has become an immensely complicated affair. We need to remind ourselves of the divine anger which our Lord reserved for those who made religion unlovely and inhuman for simple people.

The Englishman, unless I am gravely mistaken, has no desire for a religion that has mislaid its severity, he knows that he is an obstinate sinner, who cannot be rescued by methods that are merely bright and breezy. He is remarkably reverent-minded and does not expect religion to be anything but a serious affair, but he rightly requires it to be level with his understanding. Would not the simplification of our complicated Christianity be according to the mind of Christ, Who, in His earthly pilgrimage, strove vehemently to deliver the hungry from the indigestible subtleties of their professional teachers?

To-day the manner in which churches and their adherents address those who are without, and yet may not be said to have turned their backs on God and goodness, is often enough so technical, so inhuman, so loveless that the plain man simply does not know what they are getting at or talking about. It is to an adventure in a certain way of living, and not to an intellectual orthodoxy that the Churches must summon mankind; that will always be understood. As it is, Lazarus at the gate of Dives is scarcely more pathetic than the average man listening to religious instruction, or attempting to tackle the religious literature that is suggested for his edification.

For many months now the Editor of the *Sunday Express* has allowed me to address his vast and undoubtedly unecclesiastical public Sunday by Sunday. It has been as great a privilege and opportunity as was ever put in my way, and the friendships that have come out of the venture have not only been immensely welcome, but powerfully instructive to a man in my profession. I have tried to have my say without concealing the belief that, if it does not take much of a man to be a Christian, it will take all that there is of him. I have not attempted to reduce what seems to me the content of the Gospel, but to say, in language that comes easily to one who has never quite found his ecclesiastical legs, just what I have come to believe.

Within these covers are the short articles which appeared for a year in succession. The space at my disposal, as well as the public that I was addressing, naturally precluded the matter in hand from being dealt with as fully as its importance requires, but I have thought it best to print the articles in their original form.

The correspondence that ensued week by week when these little homilies were appearing confirms the belief given by ten years of religious broadcasting—that Jesus Christ has no rival in the hearts of men. We may be frightened of following Him, disinclined to define Him, but that He has still His ancient power and His healing touch no man sensitive to the needs and aspirations of his fellows can question.

RICHARD SHEPPARD.

1, *Amen Court,*
    St. Paul's,
        London, E.C.4.

CONTENTS

[xi]

CONTENTS

I HAVE a good friend who has a passion for mushrooms, and, being a man of considerable means, he thought to cultivate them himself.

He built a glasshouse and took every step to ensure that his table should be supplied from his own estate.

But I am sorry to say something went wrong.

The mushrooms arrived in staggering numbers, but not according to plan.

There were mushrooms in the drive, mushrooms down the garden path, mushrooms in the flower beds, mushrooms in the hen-house; for all I know there were mushrooms in the boudoir; anyhow, they were almost everywhere—but hanged if there was one in the glasshouse.

Now my friend ought to have rejoiced and given thanks for the glasshouse that had wrought so great a work beyond man's comprehension, but not a bit of it.

He is a tidy man, this friend of mine, liking things docketed in neat rows, and he resents quite immensely having to shove up labels about the mushroom (*agaricus campestris*) all

[1]

over the place, even, for all I know, in the boudoir.

He required a hatch of mushrooms in the hot-house, and instead there was a hitch in the garden, and, with little enough justification, my friend put most of the blame on the glasshouse, which, of course, according to its lights, had done uncommonly well.

This parable of The Disgruntled Man and The Mushrooms lends itself to a good deal of serious thinking and for my line of thought I select a familiar text: *By their fruits ye shall know them.*

We have the highest authority for saying that by this criterion alone are things, as well as people, to be judged.

We go astray in estimating the worthwhileness of any institution or individual the moment we depart from this golden rule.

It is always necessary to insist that Christianity is also divine common sense.

The standards and counsels that it suggests are not those of a God who has strange whims and fancies, but such as commend themselves to thoughtful people.

The individuals who are accounted blessed in the Sermon on the Mount, the pure in heart, the merciful, the peacemakers are, as a fact, those whom we in our heart of hearts know to be the best people.

This needs saying, for far too many think of Christianity as of some arbitrary code of morals to which they are asked to conform with clenched teeth and insufficient reason.

Christianity is actually the way of living which every man who has not forsworn his own values would desire to practise; it is still the last word in rationality and horse-sense.

And we know our Lord was right when he declared that "every good tree bringeth forth good fruit; but a corrupt tree bringeth forth evil fruit.

"A good tree cannot bring forth evil fruit, neither can a corrupt tree bring forth good fruit. . . . Wherefore by their fruits ye shall know them."

There is nothing here that is difficult or beyond our understanding, only unfortunately it is not always the way we make our estimates.

And yet by this standard alone may things and people be judged.

Even the mushroom glasshouse will come into its own if we realize that it *did* produce the goods.

The fact that the mushrooms hatched out in

[3]

the garden and not in the glasshouse is an occasion for curiosity rather than censure: what matters is that there were mushrooms, lots of them all over the place, and they were good mushrooms even if they did not grow according to plan.

That hot-house is to be judged by its fruits, and not by the eccentric places in which they appeared.

It is a nice worth-while hot-house which no axe should be permitted to hew down.

Let me follow with the suggestion that this is the only test which should be applied to the religious institution.

We must not merely ask whether it be venerable or popular, conventional or orthodox, but whether it produces the fruits of the spirit: joy, peace, kindness, long suffering, righteousness, truth.

Do these lovely things spring up, no matter where, as a result of the institution?

A critic recently said of the Churches that all the gardeners seemed inside the glasshouses and all the fruits outside.

Well, if that is so, does it matter a great deal?

If what goes on inside has produced what is outside, I am content. But has it?

I am questioning that a great deal in these days when the Churches are evidently too timid and respectable for the fray.

It is a hard question for a parson, but I must ask it. Are the Churches justified by their fruits?

How far is the evident goodness abroad in the world the result of the Christian institution, Anglican or Free Church, or Roman?

I end with this note of interrogation, for it is high time that professing Christians thought upon this matter and received again the verdict of their Lord that things, as well as people, are to be judged not by their professions, but by their performances.

Nor does it greatly matter where those performances take place.

2

SOME time ago a youngster who lived in a mean street was having an unusually rough time. He was hero, or fool enough (which you will) to hang on to his ideals, even to his religion.

They didn't at all approve of that in the factory where he worked, and he got his daily dose of ridicule and abuse.

One day one of the crowd said to him: "You blankety fool, can't you see that if there is a God who cares tuppence for the likes of you He'd tell someone to come along and give you what you need—decent food, a bed to yourself, and at least the chance of making good."

To this the youngster replied: "I reckon He does tell someone, only someone always forgets."

None too bad an answer. I suppose the reason so many perfectly preventable evils persist at all ends of the town is because such a number of us "always forget."

It was once said about the English by a foreigner, that their main vice consisted not in doing evil but in permitting it. Certainly we

[6]

find certain social evils too unpleasant to talk about, but not too unpleasant to forget.

It seems that even our public bodies and corporations, (not excluding churches,) have a way of forgetting those whom they were called into being to remember—and save.

A hardening, inhuman process sets in, and after that the institution is liable to remember no one and nothing, except that its own life and prestige must be preserved at all costs.

Beverley Nichols recently suggested that "every discussion of poverty should *begin* with the realization of empty stomachs and squalid rooms, and should *end* with statistics," and that "all parliamentary debates on unemployment relief should be carried on in the sombre and fetid atmosphere of a Glasgow slum."

There could be no forgetting in such surroundings. We cannot all take a hand in humanizing and debunking institutions, but most of us could pull considerable weight if we would remember those whose welfare, struggle or sorrow we ought never to have forgotten.

It is just decent human understanding, not charity, that our neighbour—like ourself—needs.

The man who said indignantly: "Am I my

brother's keeper?" was a bad lot. It is a poor, ungrateful, unsocial business to be numbered among those who "always forget."

As to our institutions, even they would work well enough and remember their purpose afresh if a sufficient number of citizens cared to see that they should.

A WISE man once remarked that even sheep become beautiful to those who do not see them as so much potential mutton.

That is a profound saying, for the philosopher meant that nothing can be seen at its true worth and dignity while men look upon it as existing, first and last, for their own personal benefit.

It is fatal to look at things and people merely to discover what we are going to get out of them. If we would see what is decent and beautiful (especially in our neighbours), our approach must be with respect; with hat in hand.

In all ages men have sought even God for favours to come rather than for His real worth; that is why many have not found Him, and others find Him terribly disappointing.

He is not a consolation prize.

Somebody has said that evil did not enter the world when the first man ate an apple, but when he first began to shout: "Me, My, Mine."

The rock-bottom truth about Francis of

Assisi was not that he was poor, but that having nothing he possessed all things.

The reason more than seven hundred years after his death, that he still has the power to make new friends and disciples, is simply that his way of approach to all things, in this world and the next, was the way of respect.

Like his Master, he created goodness and beauty by finding them. Birds and beasts and humans could reveal themselves and tell him things they cannot tell us, because he never said to them: "Now *I* shall eat you up," or "Do this and do that—*for me*."

He followed the example of the Founder of Christianity—surely the most radiant man of His day?—to Whom there were no "cases," but just men, women, and children.

I wish to goodness we could approach our neighbours who serve us, without regarding them, first and last, either as existing to do our will or—dreadful phrase—to be done good to.

I wish we could take some little trouble to realize how difficult, monotonous, and ill-paid their jobs often are, and with what amazing gallantry they—especially the old—carry on.

If we did, we should soon realize how fine and brave, and even beautiful, just ordinary people can be.

The nobodies would become somebodies at

once, if we gave them half a chance of revealing themselves by seeing them at their real worth, and not in terms of their worth to us.

The moment we regard our neighbour as one who should be thoroughly glad to cater for our comfort and convenience, even if we never cease to make demands upon him, we renounce our power to see him as he is, or to hear the worth-while things he has to say.

For us he has become as plain and dead as an old leg of mutton and quite as dumb.

But the moment we look at him as a human being with cares and worries, perhaps a great deal more difficult than our own, he becomes, to us, what he actually is; a decent enough fellow, good to talk to, and even to look at; sometimes, moreover, one whose untutored wisdom has much to teach us.

If you have read as far as this, may I respectfully suggest that the next time you (and I) go shopping, or board an omnibus, or call a porter to carry our luggage, we should remember that saying about the sheep and mutton?

Heaven forfend that we should be patronizing; but with a touch of imagination we might at least see those who serve us against the background of their homes and anxieties, and wonder, not that they are impatient at our barking demands, but that they are so patient, and in spite of all, such decent, likeable, humorous people.

They have lots to say to us that we need, and even beauty to reveal if our attitude to them be respectful.

It will be a thousand pities if we are without eyes to see or ears to hear.

We have the highest authority for believing that men and women are a great deal more worth while than sheep.

THE MAN WITH THE HUMP

IT is impossible for any of us—however gallant—to insure against an occasional acute attack of depression—"the hump that is black and blue."

Sometimes there is good reason for its arrival, sometimes apparently none.

Like a London fog, it just sets in, and we cannot get outside it to where the sun is shining.

No doubt you get this depression now and then; and when it comes, don't you feel that the one visitor you dread is the well-meaning friend who will be only too glad to bustle round to brace you up and do you good?

We know his or her methods, and we cannot abide them.

Perhaps the treatment ought to help, but it doesn't.

We shall be told to count our blessings, to realize how fortunate we are compared with others, and finally, for sure, the advice will come: "pull yourself together."

This last phrase literally sends me off the deep-end. For all I know it may be usefully addressed to neurotics and others who make a hobby of their "hump," but as a method of helping those who don't lightly throw up the sponge, it's the last word in irritating futility.

If our sympathy and understanding do not prevent us from employing that phrase in the presence of those whose courage is only temporarily in eclipse, then I would have its use proscribed by the law and made a criminal offence.

To think we can help our friends when they are unusually hard pressed by reeling off conventional phrases that come out of text books hopelessly out of date, phrases like: "It is all for the best," which often it obviously isn't; or: "These things were sent to try us," which they weren't, or: "Pull yourself together," which (at the moment) we can't do, is to be dreadfully inhuman.

We may even drive those whom we wish to help to despair.

Well, but how can we be of service to any who are right up against it,—or think they are, which is just as painful—those friends who, as a rule, are brave enough, but at the moment have no kick left?

I have only space for two suggestions.

First, go and see that friend and let him (or her) say just what he will; "grouse" as he likes to his heart's content. Let him lash out as he wants to, and in any manner—however lurid.

Do not be shocked, whatever he says. Let him get his worry off his chest without interruption.

Of course he'll say absurd, exaggerated things that he will probably laugh at to-morrow.

Don't stop him; don't mind, don't cramp his style.

Safety valves do not answer back.

And when your friend has talked himself out, pass the cigarettes and have grace, and understanding sympathy enough, to exclaim with real sincerity: "Hard luck." You need not say much more.

An ounce of sympathy is sometimes worth a ton of exhortation.

Secondly: If you are fortunate enough to be able to believe both in prayer and that your friend is the child of a God as lovable as was Jesus Christ, say, not aloud, but inside, when you are with him words as simple as these: "Please give my friend fresh hope and new courage with which to carry on bravely again."

I vow that prayer will not be made in vain.

NOTHING is stranger, nothing at times is more ominous, than the credulity, amounting to gullibility, of the average citizen.

We seem capable of being stampeded into accepting almost any absurdity presented to us, provided it blares with sufficient emphasis from hoarding or platform.

The great British public will apparently believe almost anything, and buy almost anything, that its purveyors loudly announce to be good.

These are great days for voluble gas-bags. We like to boast that our neighbour must get up wonderfully early in the morning if he would catch us napping.

But as a fact most of us can be stung, good and hearty, by anyone whose promises are sufficiently high-sounding and extravagant.

I do not believe that a single day passes on which I fail to open a letter telling some pathetic story of a man (or woman) hopelessly involved in misery of one kind or another because he trusted in some person for whom there was nothing to be said except that he could shout the hind-leg off a donkey.

A wise man once declared that, in dealing with ourselves, after we have let the ape and the tiger die, there remains the donkey—a more intractable and enduring animal.

It seems a poor, mean business in these days of disillusionment to suggest that we should be critical of our neighbours, and indeed this is not my purpose.

But what I do suggest is that we should be very slow to take our loud-voiced neighbour's opinions at his own valuation, especially the counsel of those who promise us something for nothing.

When a man shouts he is generally attempting to disguise the fact that he has nothing worth while to say.

And whoever declares that if we will undertake the trifling business of kicking the bucket he will do the rest, is suggesting our funeral.

In conclusion, if I be allowed to sum up what I would like to say in a slogan, I should write:

"Beware of anyone who bounces in behind a brass band."

And I would not exclude from this counsel preachers, prophets, or politicians, or any others who endeavour to drive men and women at the bayonet's point to the acceptance of their own particular values.

[17]

Of course, they may have "the goods" and be the last word in truth, but, in so far as their recommendations are noisily and blatantly proclaimed, it would be well for their public to take a good long look before taking the good long leap from which there is no creditable retreat.

If any are inclined to say that in this there is no "uplift," may I maintain, with due deference, that many a home would be saved from financial ruin, many a human body from unnecessary suffering, and many a soul from despair if men and women would take these words of caution to heart?

If individuals would realize that noise is not synonymous with truth, and that nearly all the creative people-forces speak with gentle voices, they would be much more likely to recognize what is true; and to turn their backs on what is false.

A GREAT writer, who is also a considerable musician, told me recently that, if he were able, he would give up writing prose and attempt instead to express himself through the medium of some other art; music for preference.

"For," said he, "a musician, in a bar or two, may say what it will take an author a thousand words to say less satisfactorily."

The critic who declared that an Englishman would rather listen to Offenbach than Bach often may be allowed his little joke, and yet most of us would confess that there are occasions when good music can tell us worth-while things with a directness denied to any sequence of words.

Browning said that a musician could say more than anyone else and Bach wrote a prayer in the margin of one of his fugues and then set it to music in an effort to explain it.

This is profoundly true about religion, as any man knows who prefers—and who does not?—the sound of a carol on Christmas Day to any treatise on the Incarnation by the vicar.

Nowhere is the sheer inadequacy of words

more evident than in the presentation of Christianity.

Every Church is better than its official literature, simply because there is no such thing as a heavenly language.

Those who have seen what the saints call the beatific vision—explorers as great and greater than those who discover fresh territory—cannot find words in which to express what they have seen.

The technical language and jargon which every great cause begets becomes increasingly wearisome and irritating to the plain man: he does not know for the life of him what it is all about.

I fear the vocabulary of the conventionally religious is no exception.

Unfortunately there is scarcely a phrase current among those who support Churches that has not either been distorted by controversy, or embedded in the smoke and gas which the contending schools of thought have given off; so that many deeply religious people, and many whom the Germans call "Christians in unconsciousness," hesitate to use the approved vocabulary of religion lest they should be misunderstood and add to the existing confusion.

It's a bad and sad business: no wonder that

religious writers sometimes feel that the wealth, the simplicity, and the mysticism of Christianity might be commended more readily by art than by words.

Perhaps the satisfactory compromise would arrive if no one who was not half a poet and half a musician were permitted to deal in theology.

The Founder of Christianity was a divine artist. (Who else in that day could have made that exquisite comparison between Solomon in all his glory and the flowers of the field?)

It is a soul and not a system that we find in the words of Jesus Christ.

We shall never understand His teaching unless and until we divorce it from that sometimes terrible atmosphere of repression and severity in which mankind is accustomed to hear it proclaimed.

Our Lord was and is the Eternal Voice calling to all men everywhere, not to do awkward unnatural things—like performing animals at their tricks—so that later they may be rewarded, but to be what all men in their best moments really desire to be, sons and daughters of a God as lovable as was the father in the story of the Prodigal Son—our Father which art in Heaven.

Whatever the highbrows may say, the Christianity of Jesus Christ is more akin to a light in a cottage window on a dark night than any light that may be shed from some professorial study or lecture-room.

We must serve God with head as well as heart, but it was not of theological light that Jesus Christ was speaking when He said: "Let your light so shine before men."

Yet even as I write these simple words I realize how easily they may be misunderstood and sentimentalized.

Perhaps it is true that the height, the breadth and the depth of the love of God in Christ Jesus awaits our understanding until its dull prose becomes more like great music.

IT is well to realize that loving our neighbour does not necessarily imply liking him.

The Christian is told to love his fellows. It is desirable that he should also like them, but mercifully this is not obligatory.

As a child I worried absurdly about this problem. They told me that if I would be a little Christian I must love everybody, and when I asked if that entailed liking the arm-twisting bully next door as well as an ancient relation at the other end of the town, I was told that of course it did.

Not for many years did I discover the great and refreshing news that a Christian, when called upon to love his fellows, is asked to do something which often, happily, does include liking them, but does not of necessity involve it.

Let me explain, in case some of my readers are worried over this problem.

When words are in frequent use it seems inevitable that their meaning should be cheapened and distorted.

The great word love has had a terrible doing recently, until it is used now to signify almost anything, from mawkish amiability to a black-guard's lust; from a Knight of Chivalry to a Knave of Hearts.

Now, love is the characteristic word of Christianity, and he who would discover its true significance must learn it from the life and lips of Jesus Christ.

To Him, love was no mild benevolence—such as Nietzsche railed at—but unselfishness in the widest and wisest sense of that word.

Jesus Christ said that those who would do His will must love their neighbour (as well as God) and take up their cross, which means much the same thing.

He bade men love their fellows always, but He did not say that they must always like them.

To love is obligatory, to like is not.

It sounds a paradox, but it is really a platitude to say that it is harder "to like" than "to love," for while the latter can be acquired and foster-ed, the former is very largely beyond our control.

I do not believe we need think that Jesus Christ liked His enemies, but in so far as He died for them and cried from His cross "*Father, forgive them . . .*" He loved them perfectly—with a love passing all human understanding.

Until we learn what real love means and

[24]

entails, our world will go on bumping from the edge of one precipice to the edge of another.

If and when we do learn our lesson we shall discover that we are not called upon to like all our neighbours, but to love them, which means doing unto them what we would they should do unto us.

Herein is love.

THERE is a tale about an Edinburgh surgeon that might have been written for our learning. He was a man who devoted his life to the alleviation of suffering, but seemed strangely unmoved by any of its manifestations.

One day, after a prolonged and critical operation on a poor lad, an exhausted assistant said to him: "Man, you are an unfeeling creature."

To which the surgeon replied: "Years ago I lost my sympathy as an emotion and gained it as a principle."

As individuals we cannot be charged with lacking emotion; it would be true to say that the English are incurably sentimental.

Any appeal that is addressed to our hearts will be certain of sympathetic attention, for we are a kindly people.

But exactly what, if anything, that will mean on the morrow, when the emotion has evaporated, it would be hard to say.

For years—with special emphasis since November 11th, 1918—we have been at work

applauding every sort of Idealism, from a war-
less world to a slumless city, but if we had to
report progress we could say little except that
we are still attempting to make good by
propaganda what we have made bad by
procrastination; a favourite pastime of the
merely well-disposed.

In our religion, a somewhat patronizing if
amiable good will is evident which is peculiarly
liable to run to the barren seed of sentimentalism.

To-day we are all religious in one way or
another. We may sit loosely, if at all, to
Churches, but on the whole we favour Christianity.

It has our vote and may count on our good
will.

Occasionally we walk home from evening
service after singing our favourite hymn, in a
haze of emotion, and we feel there is much to
be urged for the established religion.

Forgive me saying that I am often tempted to
think how much more virile the Church might
become if it was confronted with a little more
persecution and a good deal less condescending
patronage.

It is not more spiritual comfort but more
spiritual discomfort that churches need.

There are occasions when I long to say to those who think to encourage us by admitting that, on the whole, they can accept the Christian faith what Carlyle once said to a young lady who told him that at last she was able to accept the universe: "Gad, you'd better."

One thing I desire to shout from the housetops to-day: Christianity is either bad and untrue or good and true. If it be bad and untrue let it be scrapped; it has haunted us far too long. If it be good and true let it be practised for all it is worth and not merely patronized.

The essential duty of every man who, to use his own expression, is "in favour of Christianity," is to harness that sentiment right away to the service of God and his fellows; which means losing his sympathy as an emotion that he may win it back as a principle.

IT would go pretty hard with most of us if we lost our sense of humour, for just now and then we must either laugh or howl.

Some people cannot laugh to-day, for there is nothing in their world to laugh about.

You cannot expect the unemployed father of a family to see anything but the grimmest humour—which is no fun at all—when he is told that many thousands of pounds are to be expended on an Eat More Bread crusade. But those whose health and work hold, may still be invited to grin as well as to bear their inflictions.

Humour can ease ugly situations, smooth rough corners, and enable men to grasp life's nettle firmly with a power that is more than human.

A good joke may be a perfect work of art, of divine service to every pilgrim on the road of life.

Why may we cry but not laugh in church, sing but not smile, look pompous but not pleased?

Except that the record of humour is not

always clean and in some of its guffawing or giggling forms still in the stage of savagery, there is no excuse for leaving it out of our religion.

Surely it is unbelievable that God lacks what so often refreshes and recreates His children; or that the Creator is without that which His creatures delight to possess.

It is to me unthinkable that Jesus Christ, who told stories so charmingly, refrained from making children laugh, or that there was no playfulness in His speech when, for instance, He described the camel, hump and all, sliding unnoticed down the throat of the Pharisee.

Did no one in the crowd smile?

Laughter may be cruel and unspeakably ugly, but humour is divinely useful—a perfect work of art, so far as it goes.

There is a little prayer I use every day of my life that was originally an exquisite joke, consciously or unconsciously made.

It is the best modern prayer I know.

The joke may be familiar, but, as the prayer is not, I ask leave to tell them both.

In Mesopotamia during the war a certain soldier who was up to his neck in dirt and danger, received a letter from home of a nasty, nagging and unpleasant character.

[30]

It was the fair limit—more than human nature, in circumstances so horrible, could stand.

Back went an answer which, after asking that he might never again receive such an epistle, ended with this naïve and delightful request:—

"For God's sake, let me enjoy this 'ere war in peace."

If you know a better prayer for what we all need, internal peace, even if there must be external tumult, I should be glad to know of it.

Let me enjoy this 'ere war in peace. Life still is, and always will be, a war for most of us, but the Father of Jesus Christ can give the Peace that passeth all understanding with which we may carry on even happily. It is through, not from, trouble that we need to be saved.

IN the war all sorts of phrases and slogans were coined for our encouragement, and a perfect plague of prophets, minor and minimus, mostly minimus, foretold splendid days of lotus-eating ahead for those who would persevere a little longer in killing or being killed.

One prophecy, however, has certainly come true: the man who in 1916 announced that we were "engaged in creating a world fit for heroes to live in" got a bull's-eye, even if not the one he aimed at.

Undoubtedly our present world is eminently fit for heroes, since nobody except the heroic can hope to keep going within it for long.

This post-war world is no place for men and women who have lost or mislaid their courage.

Perhaps in every age man has thought his generation more hardly used than any other. I fancy our rude forefathers, who, we are told, painted themselves with woad (though, I suspect, they were really blue with cold), had much more to put up with than we have, but to us it often seems as if the trials of this present time are up to the limit of human endurance.

Courage is now our supreme need, for without it we cannot stay the course.

"There is a dream of human progress," writes Prof. L. P. Jacks, "which makes it consist in a gradual easing of the lot of man, in the gradual lightening of his task until the last straw of difficulty has been lifted out of his path, the last peril extinguished, the last lee-shore weathered and all is smooth sailing for ever after. May it never come true! Man is not made to live under these conditions, the lines on which he is built are far too high and large."*

In the heart of each of us there is both a hero and a coward, and what matters first and last is that the hero should triumph over the coward.

If any man can help us here let him declare his gospel, that we may hear and test its power.

There is a patriotism of time as well as of country, and every fearless citizen owes his generation the courage of his own faith and convictions.

In this matter of courage the one essential—the one decisive factor—is the question of our vitality, for according to our vitality shall we win through with credit.

To any teacher, old or new, who can give us life, and more life, we shall be eternally in debt.

*Realities and Shams. *Hodder & Stoughton.*

If there be a gracious promise that Jesus Christ in honour is bound to fulfil, it is His incomparable one: "I am come that they might have life and have it more abundantly."

Here—so Christians say—is the hidden and unfailing source of power.

Those who seek vitality from Christ, with the same diligence with which others seek fame or wealth, cannot conceivably come away empty-handed.

I read recently of a young invalid who, because she had been on that quest, was heard to exclaim: "Once I wondered how I could make the best of it; now I wonder how I can make the most of it."

It is a far cry from a city tenement to-day to New Testament times, but a great Christian, then in the midst of incredible trials, once cried: "I can do all things through Christ which strengtheneth me."

And he certainly did.

The courage of many to-day is strained beyond measure; but there is reinforcement at hand, there is life, and more life—an over-flowing vitality—here and now for those who will put themselves within the range of Christian experience.

Perfect love casteth out fear.

THE question of whether it is desirable that churches should be better attended on Sundays depends, of course, on the quality of the religion they present.

This problem was sympathetically discussed, not so very long ago, in the leading column of a daily newspaper, and the article concluded with the suggestion that if the churches are to be attractive, and attendance at them increased, there must be "a new tremendous effort to prove that they stand for what they profess— for peace and good will, for loving kindness and *for no compromise* (my italics) with the countering forces of war, brutality, and oppression."

Few who know their way about organized religion will dispute the need for this "new tremendous effort," but they may question if the result would fill the churches.

I am inclined to think that if organized Christianity went "all out" for the religion of Jesus Christ the churches would be a great deal emptier than they are now.

What I have to say is not intended as a censure on my neighbour, for we are all involved in this grave problem, and which of us to-day is willing to cast a stone at our fellows?

I yield to none in my belief in the goodness of ordinary people, but I fancy most of us still fail to realize that the Christian religion is a terrific, lovely, explosive, world-shattering force, and not an anodyne against life's little or large disturbances.

The "Magnificat" is as much more revolutionary as it is more beautiful than "The Red Flag," and it is only because we sing it without thought that we fail to realize the fact.

When Christianity was perfectly presented "many went back and walked no more with Him;" and if to-day the loving, charitable flaming awe-ful Word of God were cried aloud in the churches, there would be no shambles at their doors on the part of those who sought admission.

My desire is not to dogmatize, but (if I may) to induce people to think about religion.

It will be a painful process for all of us, for as a wise man once said: "When we learn something new it always seems at first as if we had lost something old."

In the matter of Christianity I suggest that it is high time that we all—not excluding parsons—should determine whether we desire and would support a Christian Church that would risk and give its life, as its Lord did; rather than compromise with the will of God, or whether we should prefer some mild and manageable version of religion that would be willing to make us comfortable and call our pagan emotions by gentle names: our hatred of others, passion for righteousness; our denominational preferences, eternal truth; our lust for revenge, zeal for justice; our pride, proper self-respect; our cowardice and lack of passion, statesmanlike caution and wisdom; our abominable lethargy in the face of perfectly preventable evils, the recognition that only fools step in where angels fear to tread; and, lastly, our sin, the unavoidable accident of daily living.

If in our immediate neighbourhood we had opportunity to support one of these two so-called presentations of Christianity, which (if either) should we choose?

I do not think it would be an exaggeration to suggest that the future of civilization depends on man's answer to this mighty problem.

ONE of my Sunday jobs many years ago was to stand on a tub in Victoria Park and attempt to defend Christianity against all comers.

It was an inconclusive business, as arguing about religion always will be, for "Christianity is not taught, but caught," as Dean Inge has reminded us.

If anything emerged from that ancient war of words, it was the somewhat obvious fact that the greatest of all religious problems is the unsatisfactory lives of professing Christians.

This very simple thought is addressed primarily as a reminder to its writer and other professing Christians of the extent to which their religion is in their power.

If we are able to roll away the stone that our Lord may stride forth, we are also able to crucify Him afresh.

We may declare with justice that it is monstrous that the truth about Christianity should depend upon the quality of one witness; but we had better realize that in this imperfect world that is what actually happens.

[38]

Men accept or reject Christ according to what they see in the lives of those who proclaim Him.

Perhaps, after all, it is scarcely extraordinary that the doctor should be asked to thrive on his own remedies. As a fact, it is never the sworn enemies, but always the friends, of Christ who have the power to betray Him effectively.

Those only who know Him as intimates can give Him completely away. Who but a friend, a disciple—Judas, for instance—could have led that band of soldiers in the dark, across the brook Kedron, to the secret haunt where the Victim was at prayer in the Garden of Gethsemane?

It needed an intimate to give that kiss of betrayal, and, though it is the fashion now to think kindly about Judas, I doubt if he thought kindly about himself.

To-day it is still true that Jesus Christ surrenders Himself to His friends; they have the power of death or life over His gospel.

If intellectual doubt has slain its hundreds, the unsatisfactory lives of professing Christians have slain their tens of thousands.

Is it to be wondered that we sometimes re-echo the fear of a great disciple lest having preached to others we ourselves may be castaways?

For, indeed, what men are will always speak louder than what they say.

But there is another side of the question.

May I interject one word to the lighthearted, if thorough-going, critic of the religious—the type that, so far as one may discover, is not himself very conspicuous in work for the common weal?

Is it possible for you, my friend, to go a bit easier with your sweeping condemnations? Need you lump all the would-be loyal servants of Christ together under your slashing titles of humbugs and hypocrites ("those damned Pharisees who for all their psalm-singing are no better than their neighbours")?

Men and women are not necessarily hypocrites if they fail again and again in the highest of all endeavours.

Maybe their broken bodies are more honourable than the whole skins of those who have never dared the storm.

I do not think you will find many complacent Christians to-day. Rather, I fancy, we are dreadfully aware of our shortcomings, yet eager for another attempt to make good, to make better.

If you can, ration your fault-finding, unless, with rather more knowledge than you now possess, you discover that we have no intention of meaning business.

Even professing Christians, even we who sometimes feel the guilt of Judas, could do with a little encouragement.

If you knew how great the shame is when we have failed and betrayed our Lord, you would be more inclined to weep with us than to point the finger of scorn.

It is not the part of a grown man to discourage any of his fellows who, with many a setback, are still pursuing a great ideal, that they may cry back "Courage!" to those that come after.

Nor have I observed, in those who are working at full stretch for humanity, any desire to sneer at other pilgrims who, on paths untrodden by them, are yet travelling hopefully towards the same goal.

THE English are essentially reverent-minded and do not expect religion to be anything but a serious affair.

They have no preference for stunting Churches or parsons "playing to the gallery."

Even if they had their preference should not be encouraged.

Better shut the churches and stone the prophets than suffer them to compete for popularity with the local cinema or other places of entertainment.

No great cause can hope for long to hold the allegiance of the virile that in a desire, however amiable, to win converts makes light of its essential notes of sternness and urgency.

This is supremely true about Christianity, and fortunately the Englishman is perfectly aware of it. Unless I am gravely mistaken, when he attends church he does not really require what is merely bright and breezy, but something strong and manifestly sincere; in form, dignified; in content, charitable; in expression, level with his understanding; in length, merciful.

He will not even object to what is called

mysticism, provided he be convinced that something wholly worth while is going forward.

And yet before the ink dries on that last sentence, let me rush on to plead, with all the force of which I am capable, for the drastic and immediate simplification of official Christianity.

It is monstrous that we should have suffered it to become as complicated as it now is.

It is an adventure in living, and not an intellectual orthodoxy to which the Churches should summon mankind.

No one who has lived with his fellows in recent years can possibly suggest that they have turned their backs on God and goodness; if they are ceasing to attend churches, and they certainly are, may it not be because of what is best, not because of what is worst, in them?

Men and women are finding it increasingly hard to believe that the Pearl of infinite price can be hidden within that dry, dull and dusty field of loveless inhuman orthodoxy in which they are so often bidden to seek it.

To-day the religion of the Churches has become so highly complicated, so largely academic, so much at the mercy of its experts with their technical terms, that plain folk just don't know what to make of it, what it is all about.

As well expect a new-born baby to thrive on a lump of ice as a stranger to feel at home and find his Lord in the atmosphere of some churches and chapels.

Here, scores of religious people will wish to say to me with indignation: "Even if this be true—and we deny it—why write about it— why bring your soiled linen for the public to gaze upon?"

To this I am obliged to answer that I am now, alas, convinced that there are certain scandals so ominous, and to which we have become so accustomed, that they will never be attended to until they are dragged into the market-place for inspection.

If there be any greater scandal in these grave days than that of freezing over a way by which the Saviour and Lover of Men could come again, compellingly to call His own to save their world and follow Him in incorruptness, I know it not.

The most enheartening sound that could be heard in the land to-day would be that of the coming together of all the religious; leaders, parsons, and people, that they might consider an agenda on which one item only appeared:—

"To make the religion of Jesus Christ and its official presentation—with the Cross at its centre—simpler, larger, more charitable, more human, so that all men of good will everywhere might hear in their own tongue the wonderful works of God."

I would turn the key on the religions and keep them at it until they had solved this problem, which is perfectly soluble, save for the hardness of our hearts.

Would not this simplification of Christianity be according to the mind of Christ, Who, in His earthly pilgrimage, strove passionately and persistently to deliver the hungry crowd from the indigestible subtleties of many of their professional teachers?

THERE is an old legend which tells of certain angels who had fallen from their high estate. When asked what they missed most now in their earth-bound existence, they replied: "The sound of the trumpets in the morning."

We do not need to have passed through an exactly similar experience to grasp the truth and poignancy of that expression.

We, too, in our lesser degree, have travelled that way; we, too, once endeavoured to live on the heights.

For a time we found the air more bracing, less foggy than it was on the lower slopes; but, somehow, we also failed to remain at that high elevation.

Now, in the shadows, it would be hard to discover a phrase that could more aptly describe what we miss than "the sound of the trumpets in the morning."

Nothing seems worth while. We travel neither hopefully nor happily any longer.

With no desire to make elaborate excuse for our failure, we may yet declare, with justification, that these are especially difficult days for idealism.

[46]

To those—usually the comfortably circum-
stanced—who tell us that it is "an interesting
time in which to be alive," we are sometimes
tempted to reply in words ascribed to Dean
Inge: "Yes, no doubt the Gadarene swine may
have thought the first part of their run interesting. The last part was not, for them."

The plain, unvarnished fact is that we are,
temporarily at any rate, a disillusioned people:
disillusioned with ourselves ("The good that
we would we do not, and the evil that we would
not, that we do") and disillusioned with our
leaders.

Like grit in the wheel, disillusionment has
worked its way into our moral machinery, and
is holding up our recovery.

Nothing reflects the mood of a people more
accurately than the work of its popular cartoon-
ists.

It is highly significant of our post-war
mentality that Low, Strube and Poy either
reduce their victims to mean and pigmy stature
or make play with careworn and haggard little
people.

There is a halt in human progress. Signs are
not wanting that we may soon be on the march
again; but it has been, and it still is, a lean
time for Utopians.

"Before the magnitude of the tasks ahead of

us," writes Sir Arthur Salter—no mean judge of our condition—"man's spirit has for the moment faltered and his vision contracted."

It is here that we must prove our greatness, our courage; here is the dragon for our St. George.

Why are not we who call ourselves Christians more explicitly daring and revolutionary? Why are we such ordinary easy-going people just like everybody else?

Everything that we profess and creedally express commits us to a revolutionary life.

Is it unthinkable that we should recapture our sense of decision, of daring, and urgency, and hear again the summons of the spiritual world— the sound of the trumpets in the morning?

Certain it is that not even the walls of disillusionment will dissolve at the sound of our quiet fluting.

But for the moment, gentle reader, cease to upbraid us for the poverty of our achievement and consider, instead, the greatness and daring of the Christian gospel.

Have you anything to exchange for this— the Fatherhood of God, the friendship of Jesus Christ, the sovereignty of righteousness, the law of love, the glory of service, the coming of the Kingdom, the eternal hope?

Was there ever a greater interpretation of life?

Can all the wisdom of this world produce anything nearer to the yearnings of a hard-pressed people?

There is no better way in which men and women could employ their time to-day than in asking God to give them courage, vision, and faith to aspire afresh or anew to the heights, where the sound of the trumpets is heard and the supernal relevance of the religion of Jesus Christ is made evident.

MANY excellent people suffer themselves to be overawed by sayings, called axioms, saws, even truisms, which are just sufficiently true to be dangerously deceptive.

We allow those sayings to close and clinch argument—like old Euclid's Q.E.D.

My concern now is with that hoary old saw about the unchangeableness of human nature. In its smug and accepted form—"You cannot change human nature"—it is not only untrue, but arrant nonsense besides.

We use it as a cloak for our lusts, for sins of commission, and equally for the blistering sins of omission which permit perfectly remediable evils to flourish.

"You cannot change human nature," and therefore wars, unemployment, slums, graft, exploitation and every other iniquity must continue until the crack of doom.

If men, women and children are damned of body and soul by the conditions under which they live and work, it is highly regrettable—a great pity—"but," so the pompous gas-bag continues, "I'm a realist, I am, not like those blankety dreamers; I take *facts* into consideration, I do, and I tell you that human nature never alters, never changes. So that's that"—Q.E.D.

Are we to sit quiet under this paralysing stuff about the unchangeableness of human nature? God forbid.

But what is the answer?

Will those who know forgive me suggesting a line to any who may be puzzled? If my prescription be condensed, as the space at my disposal entails, it can yet be made up powerfully for those who will receive it into their systems.

May I suggest to any who are worried by the old saying about human nature that:

(1) When you hear men say: "You cannot change human nature," you should ask politely but firmly what the dickens is actually meant by that phrase? I do not fancy they will have any rejoinder to make except that human conduct and behaviour never change, which, of course, is frankly a lie.

(2) Remind them of such old-fashioned trifles as cannibalism, slavery, torture, duelling. What has happened to them and why?

(3) You may now desire to touch upon

experience in your lifetime, of the growth of
sobriety, of the more understanding attitude
towards children, of the more humane treatment of criminals, and of the kindlier behaviour
towards animals. However these results have
been obtained, it cannot be denied by anyone
outside Bedlam that they have happened because what is called human nature has changed.
We are not what we were.

(4) How about suggesting next that human
conduct is so plastic that it can be, and is,
moulded almost out of recognition by individuals as well as by institutions, by prophets,
parsons, physicians, professors, philanthropists,
politicians, and even by policemen?

(5) Here let me slip in a caution. You will
be careful to admit frankly and fearlessly that
"human nature" may alter for the worse, as
well as for the better, while remembering that
on this occasion you are not dealing with the
question of its direction, but whether or not it
can change and be directed.

(6) Lastly: You will not make light of what
it costs a man or a nation to alter habits, or fail
to acknowledge that when you and I have
driven out the tiger and the ape from within

us that intractable animal the donkey—as was once suggested—may still survive.

It will generally be found that all who wish to lend a hand are singularly like-minded whatever creed they profess. If Christians once got going and busy they could soon tear out by the roots those crimes that now disgrace our civilization.

It is unthinkable that they should be over-awed any longer by that old bogey about human nature being unchangeable. One breath of the spirit of our Lord, and even of common sense, would blast it sky-high.

"IT is extraordinary," writes one of our leading statesmen, "how rarely in history have victors been capable of turning in a flash to all those absolutely different processes of action, to that utterly different mood which alone can secure by generosity what they have gained by force."

Fine and true as that sounds, there is nothing much to it. It is neither extraordinary nor surprising that men should be unable to walk straight out of war into peace. It is only natural.

When millions who have been permitted and encouraged to hate, then proceed with every devilish device at their disposal to work out that hatred on their fellows of another breed, we can hardly expect them to emerge from their hell as young angels of love and light.

If men prepare for war there is bound to be an unholy row.

Hear what one, whom none can accuse of being a sentimentalist, has to say about the horrors of the world war.

These are the moving words of Mr. Winston Churchill:—

"Every effort was made to starve whole

nations into submission without regard to age or sex. Cities and monuments were smashed by artillery. Bombs from the air were cast down indiscriminately. Poisoned gas in many forms stifled or scarred the soldiers. Liquid fire was projected upon their bodies. Men fell from the air in flames or were smothered, often slowly, in the dark recesses of the sea. . . .

"When all was over, torture and cannibalism were the only two expedients that the civilized, scientific, Christian States had been able to deny themselves, and these were of doubtful utility."*

I should wish those words writ in letters of gold in every school and every language throughout the civilized world.

And yet the happenings of 1914—1918 were a mere bagatelle to what would happen next time; but on this subject I would say nothing, for I detest the method—too often employed—that tries to make peace by putting the fear, not of God, but of man, into the hearts of timid people.

It is only very brave men that can make and keep peace; passionate, strong, healthy, laughing warriors—the sort that come into our mind each November 11th in the eleven o'clock Silence; the sort that hated killing, but had to

*"The World Crisis." *Thornton Butterworth.*

[55]

kill, and came back, sometimes, to wish they, too, were dead.

You may answer: "Stop all these platitudes. Who wants war?"

No one, thank God! Yet listen.

It has been declared that among the countless million citizens of all the enlightened nations of the world there could not be found as many hundreds to declare in favour of modern war as a reasonable means of settling disputes between the nations.

Yet the same responsible millions, ever since the disaster that converted them to this view, have been consistently overtaxing themselves in preparation for a more outrageously modern war still.

That is where we are many years after we cried aloud to God, and to those who gave all they had to give to end war: "It is finished; never again, this we swear."

If the Unknown Warrior died in vain, his the glory, ours the shame.

If he trusted that we would complete his work, and now we only serenade him with a posthumous eruption of gratitude once a year, how greatly pathetic is he, how blasphemous our G.H.Q. Community orders each November 11th!

[56]

Politicians, in their moments of insight, tell us that peace will only come when the hearts of men are changed.

After that they have nothing to say. Christians though most of them be, it would not be good form to add anything more.

It is simply "not done."

Has anybody else anything to suggest? Forgive my impertinence—I have.

Let Christ be called in, at great cost, to expel the clouds of fear and suspicion that still haunt the human heart, and make it impossible for us "to turn in a flash to all those absolutely different processes of action, to that utterly different mood" by which the peace of God may be won.

And, lastly, let those who long for the will of God to prevail go pacifist out and out, through and through, since Jesus and Jehovah cannot walk in step.

Speaking only for myself, I maintain, with my whole soul, that the Church of Christ is not worthy to represent its Lord to-day unless it declares, without any equivocation or delay, that no leader or ranker under its banner may kill his fellow, his brother. Why? One answer will suffice:

Christ would not permit it.

CHARLES II enjoyed his little joke, as befitted one who is called the Merry Monarch.

It is related that on a certain occasion he worried the Royal Society nearly out of their wits by demanding an explanation of why a dead fish is heavier than a live one.

With great ingenuity they worked at the problem for months, but still the answer eluded them.

Suddenly, however, it occurred to one of their number to make sure by experiment whether the dead fish was, in fact, really the heavier; and, lo and behold, it was not!

Now this trick of the Merry Monarch is often played upon us by our minds.

We take it for granted that some alleged fact is really true, and then get busy upon inquiries that arise from it.

To-day, for instance, we assume that religion has lost its power, that Christianity no longer appeals, and so we arrive at the conclusion that our planning for the future must leave it out.

Of course, there is a grave crisis in religion—
God be praised! But when the word is used
as if the crisis ought not to exist, as if Christianity could never get to grips with mankind until
it is over, it is frankly false as well as misleading.

It will generally be found that those who talk
after this manner are not so much engaged in
bemoaning man's indifference to the religion of
Jesus Christ as in deprecating his unwillingness
to subscribe to those smaller versions of it for
which they are trustees.

Will you listen to a wise man on this subject?

"It is the fashion," writes Professor Jacks,
"to express alarm about the future of religion.
Hardly a day passes but we hear some utterance, read some document which sounds that
note. But look closely and you will often
discover that what those people are really
alarmed about is not religion itself but one or
other of the entrenched camps in which religion
has been cooped up. . . .

"And, indeed, they are not safe. There is no
place on earth where a man's soul is less safe
than when immured in one of those masterpieces
of military architecture, mostly medieval. We
live in an age of long-range artillery and of
high explosives."

Here, indeed, is the crisis at which those who

believe that there must needs be a larger, braver edition of Christianity than any that prevails at the moment will be disposed to rejoice.

Our entrenched and partial versions of Christ's teaching simply will not do. Long live "the present crisis in religion!"

It is God, not man, that shakes creeds.

It so happens that during the last dozen years I have had peculiar opportunities of coming into touch with average human nature through the privilege of religious broadcasting.

I have learned more than I taught, and one outstanding lesson has been that people are haunted by the religion of Christ, but that the appeal to denominational loyalties leaves them stone cold.

I am not here defending, merely stating this fact.

To-day men and women are coming to themselves after the insanities of recent years: they are looking back in longing to the lights of the Father's Home, where their true life belongs, and the kiss of forgiveness and the peace of fellowship await them.

We do not readily use New Testament language; we do not cry out: "I will arise and go to my Father and say unto Him. . . ." But if we meet someone who is trekking homewards from a far country we long for the courage to bear him company.

We do not question the wisdom of his choice of road; we merely regret the moral cowardice that dissuades us from a similar pilgrimage.

What the Churches tell us to think is a matter for argument and discussion; but what God in the soul tells us to do is usually too plain for man's misunderstanding.

I am inclined to believe that there is scarcely a professing Christian who fails to realize that the only reason he does not take Christ seriously as Saviour and guide is that he is afraid to: and yet I am equally certain that no man ever regretted having attempted that high task.

Here is the grave crisis in religion to-day. Hail to it and courage to us! "Lord, I believe; help Thou mine unbelief."

TEACHERS—especially of morals—should remember that their lessons will sometimes be more readily received if they are salted with humour. Here goes:—

A little old Cockney was proudly displaying his finely blooming allotment-garden to a new and somewhat pompous vicar.

Said the vicar: "Indeed, my man, it is wonderful what God consents to do in co-operation with man."

"Yus," replied the little old man, "you should 'ave seen this bloomin' bit er land lawst 'ear when Gawd 'ad it all to 'isself."

Now that was finely said. Good for the little old Cockney! And yet, of course, the vicar, in his unpalatable phrase, had also spoken truly.

Man's co-operation with God is a noble theme, but often in these days, when an excess of humility is not our besetting vice, it can be very easily overdone.

This is notably so when it is suggested that God is powerless unless we lend Him our little head or our two little hands.

God's mighty purposes and planning do not

depend on our paltry contribution, and for that we should all be devoutly thankful.

It is for our sakes, and not because without us He is helpless, that He invites us into the fellowship of His activity.

We can help, but we cannot permanently hinder. He will work with us if possible, without us if necessary.

It is the height of impertinence to presume that God is stationary until we burst into the scene.

It is true that majesty is not the only element in the Christian conception of God.

"God is Love" is our terrific belief, but that is almost meaningless unless the word God stands also for something other than love. To say that love is love is to say exactly nothing. God is much more than merely amiable, as Jesus Christ set forth in His own person.

Our response to the Christian gospel will be with joy, but also with fear.

The Father runs to us before we run to Him, but when He draws near we shall not swagger into the Presence.

Nor shall we grovel, but standing on tiptoe at our full height, with head as high as our five feet something, or nothing, will permit, we shall recognize His greatness and our littleness for which latter, one word only is apt—fear.

In that sense the fear of the Lord is not only the beginning of wisdom, but a permanent characteristic of all true religion.

This need not distress any except those who, thinking more highly of themselves than they ought to think, imagine that they can build their house on a rock, when as a fact their soil is nothing but shifting sand.

Those who know themselves may well be comforted and strengthened at the thought that in their frequent hours of failure and futility God still works, still reigns.

"While we deliberate, He reigns; when we decide wisely, He reigns; when we decide foolishly, He reigns; when we serve Him in humble loyalty, He reigns; when we serve Him self-assertively, He reigns; when we rebel and seek to withhold our service, He reigns—the Alpha and Omega, which is and which was and which is to come, the Almighty."*

It fortifies my soul to know
That though I perish Truth is so,
That, howsoe'er I stray or range,
Whate'er I do, Thou dost not change.
I steadier step when I recall
That if I slip, Thou dost not fall.

*From an address delivered by the Archbishop of York, (Dr. Temple).

WHAT most of us need is not so much to be better than we are, as to be as decent and as likeable as we used to be.

Once upon a time, as all good stories begin, we were full of the beans of idealism; with the help of the Lord we had every intention of taking the next moral wall in our stride.

But nothing has quite worked out as we foresaw; we have not arrived.

It is easy enough to find plausible excuses which friends will accept, or appear to accept; easy enough to suggest that it was circumstances, not character, that determined the way we went.

We can lie even to our diary, which refrains from answering back, but we cannot lie to our soul.

For there is a voice which men call conscience, and in moments of reflection (if any) it has a way—the brute—of saying words like these: "You can cut out most of that not-a-free-agent bunk with me. After every allowance has been made, you have done badly, and you know it."

Men at some time are masters of their fates.
The fault, dear Brutus, is not in our stars,
But in ourselves, that we are underlings.

The truth is we are not the men and women
we were. Perhaps we never quite were, but
there was a time, not so very long ago, when we
were more decent than we are now, and
intended to be more decent still.

Forgive me bursting into poetry again:—

Across the fields of yesterday
    He sometimes comes to me—
A little lad just back from play,
    The lad I used to be.

And yet he smiles so wistfully,
    Once he has crept within;
I wonder if he hopes to see
    The man I might have been.

Pretty depressing stuff all this, you say, for
reading after a day's work.

I fear that, if true, it is. And yet the first
step back or up—which you will—ought to be
fairly easy for most of us.

Decidedly it is urgent. Let me suggest it.

Don't sneer or laugh at any who are hanging
on to ideals for all they are worth, who are, in

fact, fighting as we fought in healthier, happier days. Unless you have something better to give them, for God's sake let them hold on to what they have.

There is something mean and ugly in most of us that resents our neighbour possessing what we in our heart of hearts would be only too glad to obtain again, since we once knew its value as well as its high cost.

It is often true of those who jeer, that jealousy lends them its brutal shafts of ridicule and bitter speech.

We simply cannot bear to see our neighbour doing or professing what it would be well for us and ours if we still did and professed. Down with the fellow!

That laughing philosopher Bernard Shaw says that we need not be less obsessed with a truth when we are denying it than when we are affirming it.

For all our sneers we know that a good man is the last and the best achievement of human nature; as we ought to be, and, if we had (forgive me) the guts, should and could be.

I maintain that if any man hurts or attempts to kill his neighbour's idealism, especially a youngster's, he is thoroughly contemptible, and that if he does it out of jealousy he is a loathly, pernicious fellow, a menace to righteousness.

Which of us will question the judgment of our Lord: "It were better for him that a millstone were hanged about his neck, and he cast into the sea, than that he should offend one of these little ones?"

I fancy that for many the avoidance of this offence might be the first move towards better days.

There are countless people to whom idealism would remain more possible if we took this comparatively easy step.

Mind the (first) step to-morrow!

MOST of us are prepared to carry our troubles as bravely as possible, but we really must not be asked to find them humourous.

The small boy who told his teacher that he thought he could bear his toothache but need he grin, should have been sent up a place.

Well-meaning people who bustle in at our darkest hour to do their silver-lining stunt on us are not so much philanthropists as pests.

In recent years I have come to think that the "mustn't grumble" of some hard-pressed people is as near to divine music as human speech can attain. From any temptation to suggest to the obviously brave that they should also do a bit of grinning may the Lord deliver us.

To have a friend you must be one, and much of the art of friendship consists in refraining from clumsiness in the presence of veritable suffering.

I know a man who was genuinely ill for years and is now well. Almost daily behind his locked door he cried when the dawn reminded him that yet another day had to be got through.

What that poor man suffered at the hands of some philanthropists, baffled physicians, and those psycho fellows who insisted that all he needed was a good strong dose of their particular brand of "Pull-yourself-together-old-man" only he can know.

To have that treatment superimposed on genuine ill-health until the wretched man began to believe that, after all, he might be a mere neurotic must have been hellish as well as unhelpful. He must be grinning now all right, but it's his own grin this time, and not the misfit grin that was suggested, the attempting of which nearly broke his jaw and spirit.

I suppose the real trouble is that so few of us know what it really means to be down and out in health, circumstance, or (God forfend us) both. We cannot, unless we have been there.

Healthy people do not know what illness means, and even the badly-off cannot know what a man suffers when he is out of work and has to come home of an evening to tell an under-nourished, (another way of writing half-starved), wife and children that worn boot leather is all he has to show for yet another day's trudge.

We do not know, we cannot tell, what the

extremes of suffering entail, but the danger is that we think we do, and out of that arises that dreadful clumsiness that dares to suggest that the poor patient should now begin to count his blessings and then to grin.

If we think this is sympathy and understanding, our victim will not.

Professional philanthropists, please note that though you and I may spend hours in hospitals, live in settlements, and what is called, in a bad phrase, "work among the poor," in so far as we have never been completely down and out we cannot realize what they suffer.

Sydney Smith said that he would rather meet a tiger in a dark lane than a well-meaning person who is ignorant.

As a fact, my fortunate circumstances would cause me to choose the ignorant person; but if I happened to be ill and in despair I should prefer to give the tiger a grin than accept the one which the well-meaning person would assuredly offer me.

Perhaps best would be, to be a tiger and meet a well-meaning but ignorant philanthropist in a dark lane!

This is all really grimly serious, for those of us who do not understand suffering, and think

[71]

we do, must learn to be less clumsy before we can hope to help.

I am not pleading for the sympathy that is just flabby, but only for that kind which is very real and sometimes silent, because, though it longs to help, it knows how little it can really understand.

It stands by, but never says "Grin my grin;" it only does what it can with reverence, so that the sufferer may one day find his own grin and grin it.

Here is a little prayer that might be said by many of us:—

"Give me grace to-day not to pass by suffering without some understanding and desire to help. Guard my lips from the clumsy speech that does not comprehend, and give me, if possible, more wisdom, more understanding, more strong tenderness, and the power to help."

After which I always add, because I want to: "for Jesus Christ's sake."

THERE is an efficiency that is desirable and an efficiency that is not.

There was once a philanthropic society that rightly made careful investigation before it spent money entrusted to it by the public.

It was a highly efficient affair, but one day it became so efficient that it lost its soul, and this is how it happened. An elderly woman of blameless life who had fallen on hard times required some false teeth.

The society decided that she should have them on the instalment system—not the teeth, but her weekly payments.

All went merrily for months, but a week before the last payment was due the poor old dear lost her job and could not pay the uttermost farthing.

After a solemn meeting, the society instructed an official to call round and bring the teeth back to the office!

That is funny; hideously, damnably funny, and it is the kind of thing that happens often enough when admirable ideas have to work through institutions.

With their committee, secretary, and treasurer, (especially the treasurer), they become so infernally efficient that either nothing is done or else something is done in such a loveless way that decent people would rather it had not been done at all.

There was in my youth a great man— Henry Scott Holland.

He was wont to remark that whenever he sat on a committee of efficient people he had an almost irresistible desire to burst into "I will arise and go now, and go to Innisfree," and lead the pompous committee in solemn song and dance round and round the council chamber, and so away.

Once I tried it on, but it wasn't a complete success, for we hadn't attended to the most important item on the agenda—"To arrange the date of the next meeting."

There are over-efficient people as well as societies—it is their undoing and our despair.

Their brains have gone to their head, they are just swelled out with efficiency.

Once we were glad to see them, their advice was helpful, their companionship comfortable. Now they put us right and wise all the time, that is, if they can spare us a moment.

They solve our troubles before we have time to explain them, and off they go to dragoon another awkward and raw recruit.

Let us confess that we do not even wish to see them again, in fair or foul weather.

We are tired of acting as a sounding board for their talking; weary of being only allowed and expected to say: "How splendidly efficient you are."

Of course, immensely efficient men and women are right enough in times of crisis, but for ordinary occasions, for a fireside pipe when the day's work is done, and most assuredly when the going is rough, give me the man of one talent only every time.

He at least remains human. He at least understands. Always I come back to Jesus Christ, Who I believe is the master of the art of actual living.

If only we could give up defining Him and try to follow Him, we should know Him as never before.

He was always begging people to forget their dignity and dull theories and to think in terms of men, women, and children.

He remains the one superb man of history and our acquaintance who forgot His dignity, His importance, His status, and even the day's agenda, that He might become the listener and the servant of all.

So the friend became the Saviour, and among His good words were those that promised that we *could* do as He did.

THE broad-minded are not those who hold certain views of an unorthodox and liberal character, but those who listen carefully and courteously to opinions they may not be able to share.

If this be true, most of us are still singularly narrow-minded, for seldom, if ever, do we put ourselves in the way of hearing what the opposition has to say.

If we do it is generally only for the purpose of finding fault.

Nothing is easier, or at times more tempting, than to howl down the fellow who does not agree with us—confound him—but those who seek truth, and not merely the confirmation of their own opinions and prejudices, will try the harder way of listening respectfully to every opinion that is sincerely held and logically defended.

Only in this way can we hope to attain to wisdom. Intolerance has a long history, and it is still alas! doing nicely. It is at its worst in religion.

A certain famous "heretic" is well known

to me; indeed, I owe him more than I can ever repay.

His admiration and reverence for our Lord could not be questioned. He is one of the few major prophets in the land to-day, and no modern library of religious literature is complete without some of his works.

This good man was invited to a cathedral, not to preach sectarian tenets, but to reveal God and to prophesy in His name, at which he is supremely capable. Now voices from the die-hard jungle are yapping.

He was not asked qua Unitarian, but on his merits as a wise man, to whom it would do us all good to listen.

The attitude of those who would declare that while we may admire a man's character and read his works with profit, we must stone him if he approaches a cathedral pulpit, and that his goodness and wisdom must first recast themselves in our own particular mould before they can be given a hearing there, seems to me utterly impossible and entirely un-Christian.

When I remember that years ago I heard the prime mover in this dreadful business of heresy hunting successfully howling down, with the derisive shrieks of a spoilt child, the Prime Minister of the day, who was attempting to lay a contentious but reasonable argument before

the House of Commons, I am the more convinced that we must not expect wisdom or
Christian tolerance in that quarter.

We must surely nowadays recognize that no
single Church, nor all the Churches together,
possesses a monopoly in truth.

Any truth that each holds and emphasizes is
essential to all.

Let us hold our views as tenaciously as we
may—we have no use for the tolerance of
indifference—but for God's sake let us realize
that the other fellow, travelling the same way
by another road, is not only an ally, but one
whose experience we cannot do without.

"But," say the conventional, "this invitation
to men of another denomination to preach in a
cathedral is against canon law and ecclesiastical
ruling. It is also dangerous."

To which I would answer in two words,
without desire to be flippant: "Be blowed!"
Any canon law or ecclesiastical rule, however
venerable or hallowed by custom, must go by
the board, must be smashed to atoms, if it is
out of line with the spirit of Christ.

If any Church asks: "Is this legal?" or,
"Is this customary?" or, "Is this safe?" instead
of: "What does the spirit of Christ now permit
and require?" it is not of Christ.

Is it possible that our Lord would say: "This prophet and good man may not preach in a cathedral, for his definition of Me differs from that of the Anglican Church?"

I cannot think of any better way by which we could enlarge our often narrow minds than by occasionally sitting, with respect, at the feet of our partners in other boats.

Why should not the cathedrals give us opportunity now and then? Away with this heresy hunting and the hunters' bows and arrows.

We cannot help speculating on which side of the fence Church authority will come down when later it does so officially, with the issue.*

Our hope is that we may be spared the ruling that says: "A Christian act has been done, but it must not happen again."

There has been too much of that in recent years.

*Later: This was actually what happened when the Northern Convocation censured the Bishop of Liverpool and the Dean.

[79]

THERE was once a photographer whose difficult job it was to satisfy celebrities.

Now, he was an admirable and honest fellow, and one day when an unusually tiresome woman bade him do her justice, he let fly: "Madam," said he, "it is not justice, but mercy, that you need."

I expect the poor fellow got the sack for that, but he had his hour.

I am sure, apart from our faces, it is mercy and not justice that most of us require.

The really disastrously disappointing thing about us is that while, generally speaking, we know pretty accurately what we ought to be at, without a moment's delay, if we are to do better, we are for ever postponing the task. Mark you, we should be very hurt if anyone suggested that we never should do better.

It would be most uncalled for. Of course, we shall—a little later. Herein is our need of mercy.

"Lord, make me better, but not just now," is the unconscious prayer of mankind. There is an ancient legend which tells of the devil examining his minions before sending them into the world to do their work.

"What will you tell men?" said he to the first.

"I shall say there is no God," was the reply.

"No good," said his master, "they will not believe you. And you?" he asked of another.

"I shall report that there is a God but that He does not love."

"That is not much better, for not a great many will believe that," said the devil.

"How about you, what will you say?" he asked of a third.

"I shall say," cried he, "that there is a God of Love, but that there is no hurry."

"Splendid," said the devil, "off you go."

I want to submit that there is a hurry, for most of us there is no time whatsoever to spare. Now is the time, perhaps the only time, to amend.

This drifting business is the deuce and the devil for the simple reason that we can only drift downstream. If we give ourselves a few more weeks or months before doing what we know we ought to do to-day our tasks will be almost impossible.

Man cannot stage a come-back when he has run to seed.

We all know how the daily doing of the same

little thing turns into a habit, but few of us realize that the doing of one big heroic thing may lift a life at once and for all time on to a higher plane.

I plead then for the doing to-day of that essential decent thing that we intend to do to-morrow, or some time later.

Don't laugh at this little homily even if you do not need its counsel.

It is deadly serious really, for there are homes in every town and village in England that must await the return of their romance and joy until the next step in discipline and decency is taken by someone who lives there.

"But it's impossible now," may cry some despairing people. "I'm crippled and in prison —the creeping paralysis of perpetual postponement has got me."

No, not a bit of it. Try it! Do you remember the man who was in prison and despair for years?

One day he dragged himself to the door of his cell, and behold it was unlocked and he was free.

I hope this isn't too much of a sermon, it isn't meant to be, but really, now:

"You can win, my friend, and to-day, if only you will realize that there *is* a hurry."

[82]

Those who have dared the heights in one brave leap have never regretted the venture.

They say it does not hurt as badly as we think it will.

They tell us, also—and this is incomparably good hearing—that God is faithful, Who will not suffer us to be tempted above that we are able; but will with the temptation also make a way to escape, that we may be able to escape it.

THE crowd is fickle and sometimes cheers the truth, but as a general rule it gives it a pretty wiry time.

Professor Einstein said that if two per cent. of the population of the world refused any longer to sanction war it could never happen again.

I know not if that be true, but there is no doubt that the creative ideas that have preserved or remade society have usually been born to the accompaniment of the jeers and hoots of the majority, in which, unfortunately, both Church and State have usually played their part.

Whenever a true idea has arisen that has fired the imagination of a few disinterested people there is the beginning of a victory, though the majority may deride, and the little company of original pioneers never live to see its fruits.

It would be very foolish to suggest that the majority is always wrong, but it is certain that those who desire that truth, beauty, and goodness should prevail must often be on the side of the minority.

The future of the world and its safety is in the hands of the two, and not the ninety-eight per cent.

On occasions I receive letters written in a mood of perfectly understandable disillusionment.

They are not embittered letters, nor written after the odious manner of the self-righteous who think that they alone are saved; but, for the most part, they come from simple, straightforward people who are disappointed and depressed.

Their plans and hopes have not come off. They wonder if it is any good continuing to butt their aching heads against walls that do not appear to yield so much as a dent.

The cause they have at heart seems to go back rather than forward. It is no fun being on the minority side.

"What are we among so many?" they ask.

May I make respectful and sympathetic answer with a story that recently enheartened me when the going seemed hard and scarcely worth while?

An elderly man who had spent much spare time for many years in pressing for a certain reform, believing that it would benefit humanity, was being jeered at by the crowd, by the majority, for the apparent failure of all his labour.

"How much nearer is your Utopia," cried one critic, "for all your fifty years of passionate advocacy?"

"Exactly fifty years, sir," was the reply, spoken with a smile of confidence and courtesy.

It is the courtesy quite as much as the quiet confidence that I like about that answer, for one of the dangers of being in the minority year after year is that of growing peevish and contemptuous towards the opposition.

To be confident and courteous when the crowd begins to jeer is a sure sign that the day is far from being lost. But it wants a lot of doing.

Nothing is clearer in the teaching of Jesus Christ than the call to His followers to range themselves, if needs be, on the minority side.

It is because Christians are so often now only to be found voting with the majority in the interest of the *status quo* that the cause of Christ is so misunderstood and His kingdom delayed.

The attitude that says in effect: "Let us hope that gradually and with due and careful regard to vested interests, and provided that the majority will not object, changes may be brought about," is anathema to the spirit of Christ.

He remains the greatest "Constructive Revolutionary" of all time. I dare to say that there is no great problem that confronts our individual or national life to which we cannot hear the answer of Jesus.

Most of us are perfectly well aware that the only reason why we do not follow His advice is that we are afraid to.

And assuredly one consequence of following Him would be that we should often be compelled to act and vote with the minority. And on that side there are not many mighty or great.

If we could stand there more frequently, without losing either our confidence or our temper, remembering always that the great game of living is played only for love—it would be well for our world, whose future—if it has one—will be determined not by the ninety-eight per cent, but by the two per cent.

"The Kingdom of God," said our Lord, "is like leaven, which a woman took and hid in three measures of meal, till the whole was leavened."

IT is a sad but evident fact that many a worthy cause may be held up by the fanaticism of some of its advocates.

Freaks and cranks run in and out of every forward movement, sometimes getting dreadfully in the way.

Youth—for all its idealism—is not to be captured at the sword's point. The moment the fanatic gives tongue even the well-disposed are thrown into an uncontrollable fit of opposition.

No doubt this should not be, but it is so, and in this strange world we must take account of facts.

It has been said that when once a brain has been gangrened by fanaticism there is no cure, but the greater tragedy still lies in the fact that even if that brain is calling from the side of the angels the response will be negligible and its quality poor.

I am a pacifist, and never despair of the cause until I hear the bitter speaking of some fanatics on my own side making monstrous suggestions that all the world—especially statesmen and capitalists—is working for another war.

I am a Churchman and never cease to believe that one day the Christian Society will come to life in the name of its Lord, until fate compels me to be present at a meeting of the extreme partisans of my own or some other persuasion.

Then I confess that to listen to the applause which greets the extravagances which some gangrened brain on the platform has advocated, and even dared to identify with the gospel of Jesus Christ, fills me with unutterable despair.

I am not much of a politician, having voted in my time for at least three parties in the State, and being persuaded—rightly or wrongly—that the whole political business is somewhat like choosing the window curtains for the attic while the ground floor is alight; but I do not despair of political wisdom until I hear the die-hards of every party calling each other knaves while their followers roar approval.

So we might go through the whole gamut of man's deepest interests and note how each may suffer as much from the extravagance of enthusiasts as from the craftiness of critics.

Which of us but can remember how our budding interest in some ideal was once nipped by the furious assault of one of its fanatics?

To back horses has never been one of my

temptations, not only because I do not know "a chestnut horse from a horse chestnut," but because I once lived in a very poor district where it seemed that only the "bookies" were doing nicely. But the first bet I ever had resulted from the work of a vice-president of I know not how many anti-gambling societies.

I was a lad at the time, and she was a fearsome, sulphuric old lady, but when she had done with me I sought out her ancient retainer, whom she had never subdued and scarcely ever sobered, with the request that he would place my remaining shilling on a horse. (I won!)

And here comes the moral straight from that horse's mouth.

Keen people—you who support good causes —good luck to you. Never allow your enthusiasm to flag. I repeat an earlier phrase of mine: "The future of the world lies in the keeping of the two and not the ninety-eight per cent."

It is becoming increasingly clear that it is to you, the out-and-out sort, that we must now look for help if there is to be any real revival of Christianity and decency, since it is your habit to go straight to the point without overmuch regard for argument and finesse. God bless and strengthen you.

[90]

Only remember that when you desire to encourage and enlist your fellows you will do well to temper your zeal with sympathy and understanding, as well as with reason and some humour; remember, too, that if you want to persuade youth to lend a hand in some great cause—the greatest, I think, is Christianity—it might be well to recall two words that may be read on many a matchbox, to the effect that he who desires to kindle a flame should "Rub lightly."

IN the Abbey of Mont St. Michel there is a room which, if one stands at the entrance, appears to have but one little window.

The room is flooded with light, and it seems strange that so much illumination should pour in through one small opening.

Move on into the room and it will be found that the walls are pierced with many windows and through them, invisible though they be from the door, the light is pouring in.

Now kindly remember, that although the windows let in the light, the light is more than the windows, and, further, that stewards of the light must not degrade themselves into mere admirers of the windows.

The dreadful idea that God only revealed Himself to one people, through one window, while He left all the others to perish in darkness, is now happily and finally discredited.

The judgment that one religion is true, and, therefore, every other must be false, is no longer credible.

It is the conviction of the thoughtful that God has never left Himself without witness, and that there is truth in every ennobling religion.

Each, however imperfect, is a beam of light broken from the radiant glory of Eternity. The missionary who travels to a strange land, with love and respect, to learn as well as to teach, should always be acceptable, but he who arrives contemptuously on these or other shores to bid the people unlearn all that they have ever known—under the penalty of God's displeasure—should be returned empty without delay.

If this be true, is not one religion just as good as any other?

What, for instance, has Christianity that all other religions lack?

The answer is very simple—Jesus Christ; and, as Dr. Glover has said: "men who are to treat mankind seriously must make the intellectual effort to understand the Man on Whom has been centred more of the interest and the passion of the most serious and the best of mankind than on any other."

By almost universal consent Jesus stands alone.

Men may love or hate Him, but they do it intensely. He can neither be discounted nor ridiculed, and yet if He did not speak the truth He was ridiculous and demented.

Man prophesies His death and is busy in His entombment; yet in every crisis the stone is rolled away, and Jesus Christ steps forth. He allures even when He eludes, and He never ceases to haunt the hearts of men.

Jesus Christ has little need of our small arguments. He is His own credential. He counts, not because of any official status that Christendom has given Him, but because He is what He is—more real than anyone who ever lived.

It is not merely that no man ever spoke as He spoke, but that no man ever was as He was —and is.

It is here that the profound saying: "Speak, that I may see Thee," is verified.

And what was His greatest bequest to suffering, struggling humanity?

A great kindness and courtesy to sinners, outcasts, and "untouchables?" True, He was lovely to them, so that even if they feared His white-hot purity they drew near to hear Him gladly and to delight in His presence, as they do not delight in ours.

But there was something much greater than this; we must not reduce the teaching of Jesus to a gospel of organized kindliness.

The greatest contribution that Jesus Christ gave to struggling men was His passionate belief

[94]

—in which He lived and for which He died—
that God was as lovable as the Father in His
good story of the Prodigal Son.

Now that is why we set such a vast store of
gratitude by the life and death of Jesus Christ,
and—in spite of its imperfections—even by the
window through which the Light of the World
is offered to us.

Always, always men longed to believe that the
unknown God *did* really care, and that in the
end love would prevail.

They suspected it, but it was hard to accept
and impossible of proof. Now, since Jesus cried
on the Cross: "Father, into Thy hands I commend my spirit," they have boldly decided that
they may look up and travel their pilgrimage in
good heart and hope.

And so it has come about that the triumphant
moment in the Christian assembly is when the
worshippers turn to the East and declare in
awe: "I believe in God the Father."

Thus Christianity, because of Jesus Christ,
is for the Christian supreme—the Light of the
World; and the Christian society the window
through which the Light may shine.

And yet we rejoice because there are other
windows through which may come, in various

and varied beams, the radiance of the one Light of the World.

Why in our churches do we never thank God for these? As Christians our business is to live in the Light, as members of the Christian society to see that our window does really and truthfully let in the glory of God.

If not, we must move or alter or enlarge it until it does. For this, the experience of every steward of the Light, is not to be despised.

A LETTER once came to me that compelled an answer by return. I was fearful of the task. It was from a woman, telling of the death from meningitis of a little boy of seven.

"The Lord gave and the Lord hath taken away, blessed be the name of the Lord," quoted my correspondent, and then she added, so naturally and so piteously: "Well, I fail to see it, and I won't say it—and now I suppose you are shocked."

We all receive tragic letters of this sort from time to time, and there is no sequence of words that will serve for our reply.

When a woman stands by the death-bed of her little son, there—concentrated in one room —is all the tragedy of life and death.

Death has not lost its sting nor grave its victory!

What are we to say on paper when we must reply to human documents like these? Well, however firm our own faith in the ultimate triumph of Love, let us at least understand the utter desolation with which the sufferer is confronted, and refrain from the shocking inhumanity of any clumsy expression of astonishment or surprise that faith, for the moment, is overwhelmed. Remember: "Jesus wept."

That is the shortest, if one of the loveliest verses in the New Testament. Jesus was torn with compassion at what men suffered. He raised the dead to dry a woman's tears.

Supposing our life's happiness was centred in one great love, in which, as many have, we had glimpsed for the first time the reflection of the Love of the Unknown God.

Supposing, then, that lantern unto our feet and light unto our paths to be suddenly extinguished. Would not the darkness be unfathomable and even the hope of an undefined reunion at some distant date as hopeless and unsatisfying as the famous picture which depicts a beautiful woman, seated on the sphere of the earth with blinded eyes, holding a shattered lyre and listening for the music of the one remaining string?

That picture is called "Hope," but "Despair" would do equally well.

It must not surprise us if faith crashes to despair often enough after the Angel of Death has passed by; it is no time to insist that the poor sufferer should be confident.

An old Scottish divine was once asked his opinion on the discourse of a young minister who had preached eloquently and with a wealth of detail on the happiness of the hereafter.

"It was pretty enough," said he, "but for me one steady look into the dark is worth a hundred of your farthing dips."

Doubt is inevitable, and the faith that moves mountains is on the other side of a great deal of darkness. It is faith, not doubt, that asks questions.

So, when we sit down to answer the letter of the broken-hearted, we will not sprinkle our notepaper with the phrases of conventional piety. We will not say: "No doubt there is a wise purpose in it all," nor: "Your faith must be a great consolation to you," nor—oh, no, no—"It is all for the best."

One day the sufferer may press through the darkness into the Presence, where there will be a sufficiency of light, may even be delivered from doubt by yielding to devotion, but all that we can do at the moment is to stand by with just a few words of sincere sympathy, as simple as these: "It is quite terrible for you, and your sorrow must be overwhelming."

How useless and banal those words sound! Yes, but if our eyes are dim as we write them, and if there is a prayer in our heart as we take the letter to the post, they may not be as wholly in vain as we suspect. God has a way of accepting our small offers and drawing from them food for the weary and heavy-laden.

I wrote my letter, and slipped into the envelope, on a separate page, words that were once written to someone who had lost a little son: "For the little chap himself, one who knows life can hardly be sorry. He has had his peep into the world, and seen just its sunniest hour before the shadows begin to lengthen. Well for most of us if we had been put to bed then."

SO long ago as the seventeenth century a certain Bishop Hall said that "the most useful of all books on theology would be one with the title 'De Paucitate Credendorum' (On the Fewness of the Things that a Christian Must Believe)."

It is high time that the Church should set those of its wisest scholars, whose windows are still open to the fresh air, to write that book in the plainest language, which should then be issued with full official authority.

Here I desire to get directly in the line of fire of those who train their ammunition upon any who declare that the Christianity of the Churches has become an immensely complicated affair, and needs radical and drastic simplification.

It is said that we are desirous of reducing the Gospel so that Jones and Smith, who are vaguely religious, can obtain as much of it as they want on their own terms.

It is further said that we are even ready to tear the Cross out of the Gospel if by so doing we can make it more generally acceptable.

This is monstrously unjust, since the simplification of the Gospel, which would inevitably shift the emphasis from the intellectual to the ethical, would make much larger demands on the courage of disciples.

We believe that the tendency to identify the cross of Christ with an intellectual orthodoxy of a very complicated kind, and even (as is often the case) with the little exactitudes of "Church order," has been of the greatest possible disservice to true religion.

"It is certain," writes Dean Inge, "that Christ never meant to strew intellectual difficulties of the kind with which we are familiar in the path of His disciples. . . . He bade us take up our Cross and follow Him; but the burdens heavy and grievous to be borne, which our traditionalists find on the shoulders of men and women, are not only no part of the burden of the Cross: they are a sore hindrance to many who wish to take it up."

When our Lord denounced the Pharisees He was more than morally indignant. He was æsthetically disgusted at men who were playing a little private game of their own and would lay their silly and futile burdens on simple people and make everything dry and difficult.

They would not enter the Kingdom of God nor suffer others to do so. I do not think there can be a graver indictment brought against the professionally religious than that of making the religion of Jesus Christ incomprehensible and inhuman to simple people; and if that be called "emphasizing the centrality of the Cross" it is a blasphemy against the Holy Spirit of God.

Our Lord desired to simplify, not to complicate religion; to assist, not to perplex; to enable men to break out, not to break them in; but it seems that ever since His time the corporations that profess to extend His works have decided that His message needs intellectualizing if it is to be preserved, and His offer of freedom needs conditioning since He cannot really have meant what He said.

I am under no delusion that Christianity can ever be acceptable to all. I have no faith in the existence of that great crowd which, some genial optimists encourage us to believe, is only waiting to give its enthusiasm to the Church until certain ecclesiastical reforms are brought about.

We who long for the radical simplification of our religion are aware that if Christianity were set out before men in all its original freshness it would scare the life out of most of us, and put the fear of God into our hearts, and into the hearts of

[103]

all men everywhere; for then at last we should see "the centrality of the Cross of Christ."

What would be the response? God alone knows, but this at least is true: there would no longer be any opposition arising from the finer elements in human nature, which is now so distressing a factor in the world's attitude towards organic Christianity.

Until the religion of the Churches is simplified, until men and women are told officially that the following of Jesus Christ in incorruptness is the beginning, and may even be the end, of religion for ordinary people, it will not be known if the world is prepared to accept or reject the Gospel.

At the moment the plain man does not know what it is. An immense revolution on the part of the Christian Church is essential if the common and uncommon people are again to hear Christ gladly, but with fear.

As a preliminary, let the Church of England put in hand without delay "the most useful of all books on theology—'De Paucitate Credendorum' (On the Fewness of the Things that a Christian Must Believe)."

ONCE upon a time a disciple of a Persian philosopher inquired of his master where lasting happiness could be found.

He was bidden to seek out a truly happy man and borrow his shirt.

Off went the youth, but when at long last the inhabitants of a distant village pointed out the object of his quest he turned sorrowfully homeward, for he perceived from a distance that the truly happy man was without a shirt!

Now, I do not believe that the half of this story is told, for not even an ancient philosopher could suggest that he only is happy who hasn't a shirt to his back.

Man wants but little here below (as the hymn says), but he wants it weekly, and even the fool who puts his last shirt on a horse has hopes of several shirts to come.

Mark Twain once said that he had had "a wonderful education, but the worst of it is that so much of it wasn't so."

Teachers have a way of only taking what they require from the wisdom of the past and leaving the rest in oblivion, and I suspect that this story about the philosopher has met the same fate at the hands of those who, from within their comfortable shirt, teach the blessings of poverty to the dreadfully poor and dispossessed.

I fancy that only one-half of the tale has been told, and I propose to complete it.

Now when the disciple turned sorrowfully homeward the truly happy man came up with him—his chest all sparkling in the sun.

"Why do you weep, young man?" asked he.

"Why should I not weep, seeing that you are without a shirt?" replied the youth.

"Stuff and nonsense," cried the happy man, "I have a perfectly good shirt at home, and the only reason why you see me without it is that I have taken it off to do a job of work, at which I propose to sing. If you too would be perfectly happy, you will take off your shirt, and, instead of putting mine on, get busy alongside of me."

That I believe to be the full story which we should do well to receive. The difference between yesterday and to-day is largely one of shirts.

When I was young we were told to take off our shirt. Now it seems that our main concern should be to put one on, black, green, blue, white, or any old colour.

We are to be known by our shirts.

"What England wants," said yet another

man, "is a Man"—a superman, and, of course, in a shirt.

Well, well, I wonder. I am inclined to think that what England wants is not a superman in a shirt, but a million or so more ordinary men prepared to take their shirts off.

Along this unromantic road alone lies happiness and prosperity; and the devastating misery of unemployment consists in the denial of both to the nation and the individual.

What we need is a steady supply of honest, plain-sailing men and women, who can be safely entrusted with small sums, and who will do what in them lies to maintain the dignity of labour, the honour of the various professions, and to claim for every child in the rising generation adequate education, physical, mental and spiritual; the decencies of home life, green places in which to play; and reasonable security against standing all day idle, when school days are over, because no man hath hired him.

It is bravery, charity, compassion, truth and honour, loyalty and hard work, each man at his post, with his shirt off, that will make this planet happy and habitable.

For all I know, a superman might be serviceable, but I fancy we had better proceed on the belief that there are no great men, but only some millions of ordinary people who can improve their world just as fast as, and no faster than, they can improve themselves.

And the best time to begin the improvement is now, and the best way to begin is to begin.

This is a sermon for those who having ears to hear and eyes to see know the things that belong to their peace:

. . . . The healing of the world
Is in its nameless Saints. Each separate star
Seems nothing, but a myriad scattered stars
Break up the night, and make it beautiful.

"YOU—parsons are just doping yourselves and trying to dope us. Chuck it!" So wrote a correspondent to me recently.

When we are criticized, our instinct is to dash across the road and dot the fellow one, but the wiser part is to consider what truth there is in the criticism.

Is the Christian religion so much dope? This is now the commonest and the subtlest charge that is brought against it, and it is not to be dismissed by scoring a few debating points.

It is said that religion is a comforting illusion that man has invented to keep his head above the waters.

Finding himself in a cruel and impossible world, he has created God as a consolation prize, and the result is the anæsthetic that enables him to undergo the painful operation of living.

The thorough-going materialist assumes that "life is a nightmare between two nothings."

The assumption is so vast and naïve that those who are anxious to dispel illusion might find their mission here. There are not as many giants in the path as there once were.

"We now know too much about matter to be materialists," wrote Arthur Balfour, and more modern is the testimony of a great scientist—Professor Jeans: "The universe seems to be nearer to a great thought than a great machine."

But there is a certain substance in the charge, for much that now passes muster for religion is so drenched with self-regard that it is scarcely to be distinguished from dope.

God, for many, is what they want Him to be; admirable in proportion as He is useful for winning battles, assisting economic recovery, confounding the politics of the opposition, or crying up summer skies and happy days.

If the volcanic Deity of our Calvinistic and Puritan forefathers is no longer credible the pendulum has swung over far; for *le bon Dieu* of modern sentimentalism, who does not seem to mind what we do, provided we are all jolly together, is a dangerous illusion that bears no relationship to the God of Jesus Christ. This very broad-minded God, who is morally a little lax, may be a soporific, but he is certainly no Saviour.

"God is friendly—a hearty welcome to all"—
that is a good enough start, but if the preacher
ends here he is like the lover in the story, who
loved his mistress with such passionate ecstasy
that he fed her on nothing but moonshine, with
disastrous consequences. God is the best Master
in the world, but He will be Master.

This accusation that Christianity is dope and
moonshine is not to be solved on paper or in
the lecture-room.

Shelley protested against the belief that the
heights of truth can be reached by an "owl-
winged faculty of calculation."

The accusation will persist until we achieve
a version of Christianity that may not be inter-
preted in terms of comfort, until—in a word—
we re-educate ourselves in the hard and happy
school of Christ.

The point is strikingly illustrated by Robert
Louis Stevenson in one of his fables, in which
three men going on a pilgrimage discuss the
grounds of their faith.

One—a priest—bases his faith on miracles,
another—a virtuous man—on metaphysics, the
third—an old rover with an axe—takes no part
in the discussion.

Suddenly one comes running who tells them
that all is lost; that the powers of darkness have

besieged the heavenly mansions; that Odin is to die and evil to triumph.

"I have been grossly deceived; all is lost," says the priest.

"I wonder if it is too late to make it up with the devil," says the virtuous man.

"At any rate, it is not too late to try," replies the priest.

Then they both ask the old man with the axe what he proposes to do.

"I am off to die with Odin," says he.

When we have carried that spirit across from the New Testament into our religion there will be neither point nor truth in the suggestion that it is merely a consoling illusion—an opiate.

Those who make it will not cut much ice.

It would come too near to accusing our Lord of retreating from reality when He stretched out His arms on the Cross.

"AND, looking up to Heaven, Jesus sighed and saith unto him, Ephphatha that is, be opened."

What is the meaning of that strange sigh that was dragged from the lips of our Lord when He healed the man who was dumb?

Is it possible that it expressed a fear at the thought of the power for evil, as well as for good, that the miracle of compassion was about to confer?

The man must be made whole, but to what purpose would he put his health?

In one respect human nature has not changed.

The tongue can be as terrible a fire, as great a world of iniquity, as restless an evil, and as full of deadly poison as when those phrases were first applied to it.

It can be, and often is, like a prairie fire, blasting everything that lies in its way, licking and blistering all that is beautiful and of good report until the whole landscape is desolation and despair.

It starts wars and rumours of wars; it drives those who are struggling to amend still further into the abyss; it destroys friendships; it sets a neighbourhood on edge, and makes the fellowship of a church a blasphemy against the charity of God.

Evil speaking is the characteristic and the vile sin of the little mind.

We have all been guilty of it, all been scorched by it, and the scars are well nigh indelible.

Of course, we ought to practise the excellent art of forgetfulness, but it is not readily acquired.

It is easier sometimes to forgive than to forget. On this matter of idle talking there is a hard saying of our Lord's, to the effect that for every idle word a man shall speak he shall be called to account thereof in the day of judgment.

At first sight those words seem to put an almost intolerable strain on the pleasantries of ordinary small talk, in which, rather naturally, we take such delight. We do so enjoy our fireside gossip.

O give me the hour that I love best,
When the heart is quite warm and the words
  quite free;
When I sit at my ease and converse with a
  friend,
Who sits at his ease and converses with me.

[114]

Must we deny ourselves this ample pleasure—these care-free hours of recreation?

Are we to become solemn men who can make no jokes, no spontaneous judgments, even with trusted intimates, lest one word should be idle?

I fear we cannot translate "idle" as harmful. Idle is what the word means, and it is used on two other occasions in the New Testament; once, of a field lying fallow, and, again, of a tree not bearing fruit.

"Every *idle* word that men shall speak, they shall give an account thereof in the day of judgment."

It seems, then, that Yea or Nay must be our vocabulary; we must never swing free, never speak unless to improve the situation.

What a dreary, dreadful prospect for a religion which professes to encourage the high spirits of the soul and whose Founder spoke with such divine spontaneity! But one moment, please.

Only a few moments before our Lord had been saying that out of the abundance of the heart the mouth speaketh.

That sounds as if speech was not always to be a deliberate draught from the well of wisdom, but might sometimes be more real, as the spontaneous overflow of the heart.

Here, I fancy, is the key to the situation. In our idle moments our chattering reveals what we really are—our talking reveals our worth.

It is then that we are justified or condemned before man and God. We may give ourselves away more completely in our off hours than we can ever give away the poor victim of our malice.

Indeed, most of us are in grave danger of giving ourselves hopelessly away on those evenings when we think we are being unusually bright and smart, for then we sparkle best at the expense of someone else.

If our tales are true they had better not be told; if false, they are damnable. And why do we almost never report the goodness that we have encountered every day in one place or another?

If we want—as, of course, we do—to enjoy our fireside gossip when the day's work is done, and to talk free, to swing free in our opinions and our judgments, we may do so to our heart's content and as long as our friends can suffer it.

But a man who does not desire to leave his character and his friends' characters in shreds behind him might well pause, before the gossip begins, to say within himself:—

"Make me a clean heart, O God, and renew a right spirit within me."

"Cast me not away from Thy presence and take not Thy Holy Spirit from me."

"O give me the comfort of Thy help again and stablish me in Thy free Spirit."

In that available Spirit a man may swing as free as ever he likes in his care-free hours, for if the heart is right the conversation will look after itself.

"For out of the abundance of the heart the mouth speaketh."

"A good man out of the good treasures of the heart bringeth forth good things; and an evil man out of the evil treasure bringeth forth evil things."

"But I say unto you, that every idle word that men shall speak, they shall give account thereof in the day of judgment."

"CAN Christianity be organized and yet retain its soul?"

"Is a Church necessary or desirable?"

Many sincerely religious people are asking these questions.

They wonder whether religion is not crushed and rendered innocuous as soon as any attempt is made to reduce it to a system.

"Has not the vital heart of the Gospel been imprisoned by its official janitors with their administrative complications and their love of status and prestige?"

There is no religious problem with which I feel a greater sympathy than this; indeed, I am sometimes tempted to answer: "Yes, it has."

Undoubtedly there is a strong case to be brought against institutional religion.

The Gospel came, an ideal message, into an un-ideal world, and, in Shakespeare's figure, it has been subdued, like the dyer's hand, to the stuff it worked in. Church history is not good reading, and to-day the genius of Christianity is scarcely at home in our church and chapel atmospheres.

Churches, when once they are established,

become stuffy and pompous, and, worst of all, they lose all courage for the fray.

The world cannot meet the wild, untameable spirit of Christianity in the open, but if it can divert it by courting its disciples, by engaging them politely in argument, by giving them vested interests and a network of intellectual and other impedimenta to defend, it will quench the fierceness of the onslaught.

Time upon time, from the age of Constantine until now, that insidious defence has prevailed; the gentler methods have drawn the sting of Christ's religion where the cruelty of persecution would have set it aflame.

And so the Gospel has been muffled and the Christ entombed again. Whenever a Church loses the hearts of the people after this manner, the disillusioned begin to ask if an institution is really necessary or even desirable.

But there is another side to the question which I beg leave to submit. It is difficult for an unprejudiced reader of the New Testament to escape the conviction that Jesus Christ desired His followers to be associated together in a fellowship and to partake of a fellowship meal.

Although the fellowships which now exist under the name of Churches cannot be thought of except as caricatures of what He desired, it does not alter the fact that an ordered society appears to have been recognized, sanctioned and approved by the Founder of Christianity.

Our Lord knew human nature perfectly, and it is unlikely that He would have failed to perceive how men require to associate with their fellows in the greatest ventures. Group-organization is still essential, and few are at their best or bravest in isolation.

There is some climbing that may be done by oneself, but when the great heights are to be attempted it is best done by those who are joined together for service and security.

The attainment of a mystical communion with the Unseen, that is independent of every conventional aid, is sufficiently distinguished to be very rare indeed, and much that passes muster for it is in reality nothing of the kind.

Souls who live an heroic spiritual life within great religious traditions may ascend farther, and with greater advantage to their neighbours, than those who try to lift themselves by clutching at their own hair.

Ideally the Church of Christ is the school of culture, the moral university and perfect home of the human race.

It takes boys and girls, men and women of all races and classes, and introduces them to history and art, to warmth and colour, to service and sacrifice, to song and laughter, and, above all, to our Lord.

It desires that they should play their own music in an orchestra whose harmonies are not of this world, and which yet can overcome this world.

Even table manners are not outside the purview of the society, for it teaches how courteous and clean its scholars should be when they draw near to their Father's board.

"Did we," it has been said, "look on the religious institution, not as an end in itself, but simply as fulfilling the functions of a home, giving shelter and nurture, opportunity of loyalty and simple service on the one hand, conserving stability on the other, then we should better appreciate its gifts to us and be more merciful to its necessary defects."

The abuses and corruptions of the Church are no argument against it unless they can be shown to be inseparable from it.

If this conception awakes any echo in the minds of those who read it, I wish to God they would take a hand—if their conscience permits—within one or another of the churches, and work there, impatiently as well as patiently, and with all the moral and social passion of which they are capable to restore and to rekindle true religion.

ONE of the most refreshing letters I ever received after broadcasting came from a schoolboy.

I had talked on man's need of encouragement, and the boy wrote as follows:—

"A wonderful thing has happened as a result of your talk. Yesterday, our form master praised our work—a thing never known before. Can't you come here and have a go in chapel at the headmaster? We might get an extra half-holiday."

I was reminded of that letter a few days ago when I overheard two men talking in an omnibus.

One said he thought his employer must be going "wonky," for he actually said "thank you" that morning, to which the other replied that anyhow *his* boss was going strong, for though he had been with him many years he'd never heard him say that.

There are numberless people in every walk and class of life who never get a word of recognition however hard they work, and that is often enough the last straw that breaks the willing back.

There is a pernicious doctrine still rife that if you give a word of praise the recipient will get above himself.

I do not know how it is with my readers, but I suspect it is much the same as with me. We'll work ourselves to the bone if now and then someone says: "Well done" or "Well tried."

But if those words are never spoken, if there is no sign that our patient slogging at the same old job is at least appreciated, it is impossible to do our best.

I suppose ideally the sense that work has been carefully done ought to be its own reward, and that may be so when work is interesting and salary and prospects good, but the majority of us don't go to the City to add up somebody else's figures, or hammer somebody else's typewriter, or invest somebody else's money for the pleasure of going to the City to do these things.

And if the monotonous jobs of men at work or women at home must be done year in and year out with never a word of cheer, life becomes pretty grim.

It was said of a certain man by one who served for years on his staff that "With —— you begin your career every morning." That may be the inspirational stuff to give the young genius, but we ordinary folk who are a bit older, a bit worried, and a bit tired cannot be expected to thrive on it.

Here is an extract from my correspondence: "If only I got an occasional pat on the back I could stick it better, but I cook and wash and nurse all day with never a kind word; once it wasn't like this, and then I enjoyed hard work."

It is sometimes suggested that it embarrasses people to be thanked, and certainly the hearty friend who is always telling us how fine our work is may be a nuisance and possibly a liar, but I know, and you know, one or two Cinderellas of both sexes who could do nicely with a little more gratitude.

They could stand a lot of so-called "embarrassment."

The sudden shock of finding one's efforts are appreciated seldom kills.

Let me tell a story that will exactly illustrate the point I desire to make. I have told it elsewhere, but it will bear repetition.

I once married a friend—a fine fellow—who belonged to the fighting forces. Early on the morning of his wedding one of his men—not of commissioned rank—arrived after travelling all night from the north of Scotland at his own charge to attend the ceremony.

When the wedding was over I asked my friend if I should fetch the traveller to be greeted by himself and the bride.

"Certainly not," said the bridegroom, "it would merely embarrass him."

I protested, but was told that "in the Service that sort of thing is not appreciated."

Later that day I found the tired guest solacing himself in the local public house. A bit fuddled on most things, he was perfectly clear on one: he would not have believed that the officer to whom he was devoted could have treated him so cruelly.

So much for the argument that it always embarrasses a faithful friend to get a thank you for services rendered.

We are not often able to assist our neighbour in ways we should wish, but the world would be different to-morrow if we had the grace to acknowledge our indebtedness to him.

Ingratitude is, indeed, a miserable business; perhaps the blackest, ugliest, and, as it is certainly, I fear, the commonest of sins.

And those to whom the sympathy of men might well go out most surely are the women who toil at home, and who are expected to be and look nice at whatever time their husbands or brothers deign to return.

I cannot agree that "every man marries above him," but I have found no cruelty more dreadful than that which the ingratitude of an unimaginative man can inflict on a woman.

It is easy to trample the romance out of a woman's heart by denying her those little courtesies that were once so gladly given, and the failure to recognize what it costs her to live and bear with us is often the first step that leads to that disaster.

If any of us would take a hand in easing the burden of our fellows we shall find no way more sure than that of giving thanks when thanks are long overdue—especially at home.

"IF Jesus came to London what would He say?" I have been asked. It is a pertinent question, but only an impertinent person would answer it with confidence.

The wise and understanding will not think that our Lord has taken them into His confidence.

They believe Him to be the same to-day as yesterday, but yesterday He both allured and eluded men, and so assuredly would it be to-day.

When He walked with His followers, He was always going on ahead of their comprehension.

They thought they understood Him, and lo! He went on in advance and they were left, amazed, afraid, baffled, and yet faintly pursuing.

It is the same to-day. We try spasmodically to catch up with Him, for His supremacy is still unquestioned, but just when we draw near He goes on ahead, in advance of our courage and understanding, and we are left, amazed, afraid, baffled, but still desiring to follow.

"A little while and ye shall not see Me; and again a little while and ye shall see Me; because I go to the Father."

How true it all is. Who would dare say with any confidence what Jesus Christ would say were He to come again?

And yet we may exercise our imagination. I do not know what our Lord would say to my neighbour or to me, but I suspect very little more than He has been saying now to both of us for many a long year; for I fancy it is only moral cowardice that causes us to declare that up to now the Christ has never communicated with us.

If He were to return in person I fancy He might only emphasize what He has been attempting to drive home to us time and time again—"Get your values right and your lives and institutions will work well enough," or "Seek ye first the Kingdom of God and his righteousness and all these things shall be added unto you."

We have often heard that counsel and we have not argued against it; we have only said it is sound advice which we propose to take at a later date.

I can fancy our Lord walking about the streets talking to anyone who would speak to Him, compelling no man to follow Him, but speaking words so real, so reasonable and so fiercely true that they would haunt for ever after.

[128]

I do not think that Jesus Christ would de-nounce London as no doubt John Baptist would.

I think He would weep over it as He wept over Jerusalem, not because He despaired of human goodness, but because even He would be almost unable to understand how people who had peace and joy within their grasp could blindly seek both in places where neither may be found.

If our Lord came to our social gatherings I do not think He would talk a great deal, but just now and then a few spontaneous words would come from the overflow of His heart. Like a strolling minstrel of genius the more inane the talking around Him the more divine would be the music that He would make.

After that I fancy many of us might seek Him out, possibly by night, and He might say to us words as strange as these: "Whosoever drinketh of this water shall thirst again; but whosoever drinketh of the water that I shall give him shall never thirst; but the water that I shall give him shall be in him a well of water springing up into Everlasting Life."

When He had spoken thus, it is likely that we should say: "I really don't understand what it is all about," or "What has it got to do with me?" and yet I think that even as we shuffled off home we should understand better than we would allow, at least as far as we ourselves were concerned.

He would have pierced our souls.

It is very hard at times to know what the Christian attitude ought to be on large questions of public concern.

Here without self-deception we may often be at a loss. The Gospels make us eager, but they do not tell us nearly enough.

They ask as many questions as they answer, and it is natural that we should long for Christ to come again in the flesh.

But I wonder whether we do not already know perfectly well what Christ would have us do in almost every given circumstance of our daily living, and I wonder too if we do not also know that we could do it, or at least attempt to do it, if we would bank on His present and ready help.

When Jesus came to Birmingham
   they simply passed Him by,
They never hurt a hair of Him,
   they merely let Him die.
For men had grown more tender
   and they would not give Him pain,
They only just passed down the street
   and left Him in the rain.

[130]

Still Jesus cried: "Forgive them,
   for they know not what they do."
And still it rained the winter rain,
   that drenched Him through and
     through,
The crowds went home and left the streets
   without a soul to see,
And Jesus crouched against a wall and
   cried for Calvary.*

*G. A. Studdert-Kennedy. ("Peace Rhymes of a Padre,"
    Hodder & Stoughton.)

IT is hard to prophesy what our Lord would say to London were He to come in the flesh, but fairly easy to guess what London would say to Him.

God alone knows what Christ would make of us, but we know pretty accurately what we should make of Him.

Undoubtedly His arrival would throw us into much the same confusion as occurred precisely at eleven o'clock on November 11th, 1918.

We should cast our work and play to the winds, leave home or office to wander among our fellows, inquiring of every passer-by what was the meaning of this portentous advent that had dawned in our winter sky.

What did it forebode? How eagerly we should await the evening papers to explain or explain Him away; doubtless the bewildered leader-writers would already be hard at work buzzing inquiries along the lines that connect Fleet Street with Lambeth.

For ourselves, we should be strangely elated and strangely confused. It would be most disintegrating, for although for years we have been asking for a man, the arrival of the One who,

by instinct rather than by orthodoxy, we have
long called The Man is surely a little sudden
and premature.

And yet without doubt He comes in the ful-
ness of time, for the world is in dire need of
repair; the voices of its chosen counsellors have
lost their ring of confidence.

But, still, earthquakes are not in our line.
Here is the setting in which the Christ is to take
the centre of the stage.

And at first all will go well. There will be an
immediate success, and if the Prophet wear an
Eastern garment we shall be the more diverted,
for we are fond of novelties in our religion.

But a check soon happens, for nothing very
startling and miraculous takes place, and the
remnant that remains is sifted and thinned still
further at the first appeal for individual righteousness.

I think that we should soon be saying that our
Lord is disappointing and curiously ineffective.

As a social reformer, He lacks a programme;
as an orator, He is unconvincing: a good man,
no doubt, but unpractical and unwise.

Obviously He loves deeply, almost desperate-
ly, but His speech is careless and too spontaneous, it lends itself to misunderstanding.

10

He talks nothing but the dialect of the human heart, very persuasively, but it is rather embarrassing, and too painfully direct. Altogether an interesting and considerable personage, but —forgive us hazarding the suggestion—is He not just a little extravagant and emotional?

And one cannot run this modern world on extravagance and emotion.

Why, once He blazed out at a number of quite excellent people who were merely tightening up their creed in the interest of religion itself, and twice He was seen to cry in public, once in Park Lane, and again in Poplar.

Clearly, too, He is no match for the learned. He will not counter their arguments with arguments of His own.

He says that it is useless to argue with those who will not unlearn, and He merely tells them to forget their dull theories and to think instead of men, women and children.

After which He passes on to a company of people who are not nearly so worth while, indeed rather a second-rate lot.

And He makes the mistake of allowing passion to creep into His message. He says that only through passion can man attain to wisdom and that God is as passionate as the Father in the story of the Prodigal Son.

He says that the cold wisdom of this world is

[134]

lunacy, and that sanity comes as surely from warmth as insanity from coldness.

He bids men be passionate, and, of course, that is a great mistake and a little dangerous.

A man whose message is coloured by his emotions is not a safe guide. And then there is one other factor, and this, I fear, is determining.

It is found that our Lord is not really English: He is not wholly devoted to our British interests.

Not being "sound" here is fatal. For some little time He has been suspect and this is just too much.

London is genuinely sorry to lose so gracious and well-meaning a figure, but it would be best for Him to leave.

Anyhow, with much courtesy we should ask our Lord to leave our coasts, for a time at any rate.

And meanwhile, to placate His strange followers, we might appoint a committee of erudite ecclesiastics, with a Privy Councillor or two and, of course, one woman and one representative of Labour to assist, to investigate with a view to obtaining from His teaching some practical scheme which would be generally acceptable for national improvement and international security.

I am not being censorious—God knows I have no right to be. But this is what I really believe London would do to our Lord.

[135]

I EXPECT most readers who do me the honour of glancing at these pages have a feeling amounting to something like pity for those who follow my profession.

It is not unnatural that this should be so, for if what the average good fellow believes about the parson's job were true we should be of all men the most pitiable.

On the afternoon of the day on which I was ordained in St. Paul's Cathedral the omnibus which was taking me to my work in Bethnal Green was boarded by two men who had done themselves proud in the dinner hour.

Said one to the other, when he caught sight of the parson: "Gawd, Bill, here's a blankety parson," to which his pal, who was carrying his liquor more genially, replied: "Nah, then, George, don't blame 'im, it ain't 'is fault, it's 'ard luck, that's what I calls it."

Of course, I laughed (who wouldn't?), but I didn't laugh deep down, for I knew then, as I know now, that no words could have explained better than that homely backchat just what the world thinks about the minister of religion.

[136]

I am not concerned here to defend my profession, still less to excuse its shortcomings, but I would like, (if I can,) to explain what we are after, so that ordinary people might make their judgments on rather better information than at the moment they possess.

Will readers bear with me while I try briefly to explain what I believe a parson is and what he is not?

I cannot speak for the Church as a whole, but I do not think that many of my colleagues in any Christian denomination would dissent from these views.

Perhaps it would be better to begin by saying what a parson is NOT.

He is *not* a man, (unless he is a complete dud,) who thinks himself better than his neighbour.

He is *not* a man who desires to lord it over his fellow-men.

He is *not* a man who is automatically preserved from religious doubt, nor from temptation that assails the flesh.

A parson has to meet nearly every temptation which other men must contend with, and there are further, reserved for him, peculiar and devastating temptations which are as subtle as the devil himself.

[137]

A parson is *not* a saint—he is a sinner like his fellows.

A parson is *not* one whose business it is to find fault in his neighbour, but one who is engaged in finding good.

He is *not* a man who believes that he is empowered from on high to dragoon men and women into the acceptance of certain traditional beliefs under pain of God's displeasure.

He does *not* desire to hurl such truth as he has received at any man's head, but, since he believes that it is vitally important, he is passionately anxious that they should consider it.

He offers what he holds respectfully and courteously to all who realize that man cannot live by bread alone.

The parson does *not* tell men that they ought to attend his church, but he desires to keep his church and himself alive unto God, and he hopes and prays that he may be allowed to give men their meat in due season.

And now what *is* a parson for? In the King's Regulations it is laid down that the job of the naval chaplain is "to be the friend and adviser of all on board."

I do not know how what is called the ministry could be better defined. Ideally the parson should be the friend and adviser, (when asked,) of all among whom he lives.

Whatever their work or circumstances, their outlook or belief, he should desire to stand by and lend hand and head.

There is no job so humble or inconspicuous, or so apparently secular that a parson may not tackle it, if by so doing it he can serve his neighbour in the spirit of Jesus Christ.

He should light fires in dark rooms, and go on lighting them all his life.

The parson is a man who is travelling hopefully. He is within the crowd, and not outside it; he is a pilgrim with all other pilgrims on the road, and not a cocksure and confident little guide going on and disappearing in the distance.

The parson desires to grow more and more in the knowledge of Jesus Christ, not for his own salvation, but that he may assist other pilgrims who have not his time or opportunity for such research.

He is one, moreover, who has every social evil—war, unemployment, slums—permanently on his conscience; he should condemn injustice and exploitation passionately and fiercely, and without compromise—even to the emptying of his church.

It is better for him to be called a "Bolshie"

and "a wild man" than to be approved of as merely an upholder of what now is in Church or State.

And the parson must be a supremely human man, unshockable, and yet hating sin. It ought not to be impossible for him to remain human if he retains a knowledge of his own weakness and remembers how hard it is for him to be a Christian.

The parson's main work is to be an expert in the art of living well and loving wisely, as was his Lord and Master.

He is here not to kill happiness or to curtail freedom, but to enable men to shoulder their burdens in good heart and courage, and to break out and through into the knowledge of God.

Above all, the minister of religion must be a man of prayer, and yet the world need not know how often, or how hard, he prays.

We should all be wiser and better if we judged a man's worth with a little more knowledge of what he is after.

We parsons ought to know better what is going forward in our neighbour's profession before we make our judgments, and the world might be a trifle more understanding of the professionally religious if it knew more about the ideals that underlie its perhaps unattractive appearance.

The parson's job is a tough one, but painfully conscious as we are of repeated failure it does seem (to us) worth while, and there are few of us who would be willing to embrace any other profession.

REALLY, some of these theologians drive one almost frantic; their minds have gone to their heads.

A guide at the Sorbonne once said:—

"This is the hall where the Doctors of Divinity have disputed for four hundred years."

"Indeed," said the visitor, "and what have they settled?"

I have nothing but respect for theology—it is essential if we would give a reason for the faith that is in us—but for some theologians I have no respect whatsoever.

I distrust them as deeply as, no doubt, they distrust me.

We are suffering severely from academic religion.

We are right to have a respect for learning, but it should be remembered that one may sometimes hear more abysmal nonsense talked in a Senior Common Room at Oxford, or Cambridge, than at a Mothers' Meeting. I am not now prepared, as I once was, to make obeisance to mere intellect. I do not think its record is creditable.

For the recovery of religion I am not looking to those theologians who do not move about among their fellows.

At the moment their verdicts receive more than their fair share of attention; we simple people suffer them to overawe us.

Of the hundreds of books on religion that are published each year the vast majority are totally unintelligible to any who have not made theology a special subject, or who are unfamiliar with religious phraseology.

There is a great deal to be said for not leaving the case for religion in the hands of theologians, for whom—with some notable exceptions—it seems that Christianity has ceased to be their love and become their business.

They are dangerous fellows; more interested in controversy than in truth. Forgive me for deep-ending like this, but I am in an unreasonable and bad temper to-day, and I should enjoy loading a ship with a number of theologians whom I could name and sending it right off to a cannibal island.

Which reminds me of a story about a cannibal king who enjoyed eating missionaries with his tea.

After repeated warnings a paternal Government sent a ship with an admiral in charge to the island to fetch the old king back to be strung up.

On the way home, the admiral and his prisoner became great friends over many a game of poker, and three days from port the cannibal was told that if he liked to escape in a boat pursuit would not be attempted.

Later, when the home authorities required the gallant admiral to explain the absence of the prisoner, he declared that after the most careful investigation he had come to the conclusion that the cannibal king was justified!

To-day I feel exactly the same about those theologians I have packed off to a cannibal island.

I do not excuse myself; of course I am wrong. No theologian, however tasty, is quite bad enough for the stewpot, but some undoubtedly should be silenced for ever.

I fancy that my nasty temper towards theologians is somewhat justified to-day. You see I have just been talking to a friend, an intelligent person, who has lately what is called "got religion."

He was going away for Whitsuntide with a bag of steel shafts, and he thought to slip into his pocket a book that would be suitable for Whit Sunday.

He paid a visit to a shop that specializes in religious literature.

There, on the counter, was evidently the book he required. It was a short book by a likeable and immensely learned professor in one of our great universities. It was about the Grace of God and the price was reasonable.

But the book has been brought to me. Ought my friend to try to understand it? he asks.

To me, who have naturally been at least grounded in theology, the book is entirely incomprehensible. It is two shillings and sixpence worth of wrinkles.

In the editorial foreword it is announced as one of a series of books that "are not technical handbooks, but aim at presenting facts intelligently to the educated public, without any sacrifice of interest and attractiveness."

This particular book has seven chapters, and here are the titles of five of them :—

"Grace" in Christian thought before St. Augustine.

Grace in St. Augustine.

Synergism.

Synergism in the Churches of the Reformation.

Post-Tridentine Catholic Synergism.

God help the keen layman. If this is not a

technical handbook, but one "that aims at presenting facts intelligently to the educated public, without any sacrifice of interest and attractiveness," then preserve us alive from the professorial production.

Let me be pardoned then for railing against those theologians who—in this day of God—think to serve the great cause of explaining the religion of Christ to plain people in such a way.

It really is time that simple people were delivered from the subtlety of some theologians.

They are making Christianity entirely ugly and inhuman. They are leaving out Jesus.

THE death of a little old man—at least he looked old—who sold newspapers in Central London, next door to the Church of St. Martin-in-the-Fields, occurred recently.

Hundreds of us knew him as "Siddie," and we bought his goods more because we were devoted to him than because we wanted to read them.

He was a tiny, crippled man with a weak chest, and he sat on a box, day in and day out, wet and fine, in as draughty a corner of the street as London can provide.

His pitch was up against the railings of a house that I lived in for years, and the sounds of "Siddie's" trading were wont to come in through the windows of the room in which I worked.

Once the noise disturbed me. I thought it harsh and raucous, but when the little man became my colleague and friend I liked it well.

In that room which was separated by only a wall from "Siddie's" old beat I miss the noise quite horribly.

For music had crept into the little cripple's shouting, so that even in the dark days of war his "Paiper! Paiper!" had taken on a sound that was for me uncommonly like "Lord, have mercy upon us; Christ, have mercy upon us! Lord, have mercy upon us," and when better days arrived he seemed to cry: "We thank Thee, O God."

This will sound absurd to those who did not know "Siddie," but the children of the neighbourhood—our village—who once subscribed to pay someone to do his job while they entertained him at "Peter Pan" will understand.

I hate the thought of their and my friend passing away without some memorial. This small tribute to the honour of a great little paper man, with crippled legs, a wheezy chest, and indomitable courage, is all he is able to have.

We could not give "Siddie" a great funeral, and I doubt if he would have wished it; we did not know of his death until after he was under the ground.

To us he said that he had comfortable quarters, and on his return to work after bouts of illness he made reference to a relation who had looked after him well. "Siddie" was splendidly proud so that we dared not investigate his circumstances.

As to his religion, well, he was a buttress

rather than a pillar of the Church, since he was always outside, and somehow though he loved the church that was hard by his pitch, and looked on those who served it as his intimates, I never wanted him inside.

I do not think church services would have helped him. "Siddie" was better as he was. Personally I had nothing to teach him, and I knew him well and had watched him in all weathers.

He did lovely things, like buying sweets for children, minding cars, and hobbling off on errands without reward, but he knew life through and through, and you couldn't sting him.

After talking with him I used sometimes to say inside myself: "Of such is the kingdom of God."

I believe "Siddie" would at times oblige his clients by putting their bobs on for them, but I know one case at least where he refused to assist a poor lad in this direction on the plea that betting was a "mug's game" for a youngster; and I remember that often in the late evening, when the music of his shouting died down for a few minutes, it was because he was telling some unfortunate man or woman who had drifted into Trafalgar Square that they could rest in that church which never shuts, or that perhaps if they knocked on the front door behind his railings some "bloke, who won't bite you," might lend a hand.

"Siddie" has gone, and I feel that the population of the world is indeed one less.

I miss him: his voice is hushed—something seems all wrong.

It is the irony and grandeur of life that always—even when we buy our newspapers—we may be entertaining and entertained by an angel unawares.

"Good luck, 'Siddie,' in the name of the Lord—we are not worrying about you, but you're missed on your old pitch."

A HAPPY home life is one of God's greatest gifts, for the memories of our childhood are coloured by the love we had shown to us then.

Some have not these happy memories, they can only recollect sadness and bickering and sometimes, perhaps, tragedy.

The other day an intelligent woman called to see me; she was splendidly happy in her present marriage, her previous matrimonial life had proved—shall I just say?—a failure, and had been dissolved; nor does it matter one little bit to the point of my story as to who was the guilty party.

There was only one little difficulty—well, perhaps not little, for so much depended upon it—both she and her husband, good Christians both of them, at least what we mean by being Christians, were desirous of making their Communion.

They felt the need to express in Holy Communion all that life now meant, and all that it ought to mean; but they had heard that no person who had been a party to a divorce

[151]

was allowed to communicate at a Christian altar.

What should they do? What did I advise?

I did not even stop to think, because I have thought so long about it. There was to me only one possible answer.

I may be quite wrong, but I felt I knew what our Lord would have me do in similar circumstances, and I gave them Communion gladly.

There was sounding in my ears what Jesus had said to the woman who was a sinner: "Go in peace."

I know the theologians and the ecclesiastics put up a great fight against divorce.

I am not sure that I advocate easier divorce; I really don't advocate it at all; for divorce really spells failure, and I am not particularly interested in advocating failure.

I only wish to help and assist those who have made a failure; and I do advocate happiness and a godly life, believing that all should have life and have it more abundantly.

Yet in those cases where marriage has proved itself not to be what the Church and God mean by marriage, I am convinced that perhaps dissolution of that legal contract may be the only means of establishing peace and good will in family life.

[152]

Words can be terrible things, but still they mean and convey something to us.

And I become so tired of all the legal and ecclesiastical quibbling: the ecclesiastics will move heaven and earth to prove that a marriage is null and void—that it is no marriage.

We have seen that time and time again, and history is full of instances, even in our own time.

With the same logical coldness it will tell you that a marriage cannot be dissolved—prove it was never a marriage, all is well, and no obstacle will be placed by the Church upon remarriage, nor are the persons excommunicated and forbidden to count themselves of the fellowship of Christ's Church.

But dissolve a marriage! No, impossible. Well, I feel somehow quite differently about it. "Go in peace"—without that we shall never get anywhere, and the problem of annulling marriages or divorce is a problem which will have to be faced while marriage exists; for marriage is a legal contract, and like all legal contracts may be broken.

Make no mistake, this is not a loosening of our social relationships, it can only be said by one who profoundly believes in marriage and all that marriage should mean.

It is not holding a brief for the sort of thing

that one hears happens in Hollywood, which is so utterly inhuman that one sometimes wonders if any of it is true.

But while human frailty permits me to marry people without considering whether they are fitted or prepared for marriage, whether they have considered all that living together and sharing a home implies, we cannot fail to see that sometimes we shall have to make adjustments.

It is only in this way that we can hope eventually to make marriage partake of that divine quality which we declare happens when we join the hands of a couple in matrimony.

I seem to have got a long way from my lady and her problem. Does the fact of her being divorced shut her out for ever from the divine grace?

Can I only give her the consolation and help of Communion after I have instructed her to leave her husband and make me a promise never to see or hear anything of him?

The law of the Church may be plain, the voice of the ecclesiastics, the College of Rites, and the bench of bishops may be unanimous, but to me the spirit of Jesus proclaims louder than any law of man, than any unanimity of the

Church, that the law of Love says to you and to me: "Go in peace."

I know, having read as far as this, some are quaking with rage at my unorthodoxy.

I shall be accused of desiring to weaken the moral code of the land; I shall be told that hard cases make bad laws—well, what of that? I dare only express what Jesus says to me, and He says it with no uncertain voice: "Go and sin no more."

At least, in my judgment, no man or woman should ever be debarred from kneeling reverently at the service which our Lord Himself founded for sinners, and not for saints.

THERE are few things more depressing to a thoughtful person than what are known as fashionable church weddings.

They are disappointing all round; disappointing for the couple to whom their marriage day is a solemn occasion; dreadful for the bridegroom who is scared stiff; irreligious for the sightseers who have come with good wishes; and devastating to any who would fain speed the bride and bridegroom on their way with prayer.

For the parson, if he be in earnest, the atmosphere of the whole business is as unseemly as a great deal of the language he is supposed to use.

The short address at the close may conceivably just rescue the ceremony from complete religious collapse, but that will depend on the man who gives it and owes nothing to the Prayer Book service.

It is true that many clergymen now use the amended form, which, to put it bluntly, is winked at by authority, but the Church is to be judged by its authorized and not by its unauthorized forms, and—so far as I know—there is not a single bishop on the bench who does not think it his duty to read every line of the service as set down in the Book of Common Prayer.

For far too long now the Church of England has been content to prescribe ceremonies for great occasions—birth, death, and marriage— which are simply not good enough.

On these occasions even those who appear to be indifferent to the higher issues of life are given pause to think.

Normally, they may be occupied only with things they can touch and see, but at these moments the mystery of life confronts them. They are carried into surroundings in which they will be peculiarly sensitive to spiritual influences.

Here, one would think, is a great opportunity for the Established Church, yet the ancient ceremonies it offers its children are unlovely and outworn.

Froude, the historian, writes: "If medicine had been regulated three hundred years ago by Act of Parliament . . . if every licensed practitioner had been compelled, under pains and penalties, to compound his drugs by the prescriptions of Henry the VIII's physician,

[157]

Dr. Butts, it is easy to conjecture in what state of health the people of this country would at present be found."

The most fundamental criticism brought against public worship to-day is that its language is aloof from the understanding of those for whom it is intended. This criticism is one to which there is no satisfactory answer.

It is nothing less than ecclesiastical Philistinism to suppose that imitation Elizabethan language is more beautiful than good honest Georgian.

Let me relieve my feelings about what may be called the Mayfair-ing of matrimony. You know what I mean—the botanical gardens background, the inane chattering, the craning necks, the attending children, disguised as courtiers and liable at any moment to burst into nursery noises, the general air of thoughtless irreverence in which it is hard to believe that anything religious is taking place.

Please hear what the late Lord Oxford and Asquith wrote to a friend about one such ceremony. "I went after lunch to St. Margaret's to the marriage of ——'s niece, who was making what is called an excellent match.

"It was a crowded fashionable function—in the worst sense. As I followed once more the familiar service, I felt all the repulsion and more that you described at ——'s wedding a couple of weeks ago.

"All the strained, unnatural metaphors about Christ and His bride the Church, the servile insincere formulæ except in the mouth of people not yet grown up; with a dreary platitudinous elocution by a minor bishop. It filled me with something like nausea."*

Which of us has not suffered a like discomfort on the occasion of a wedding?

It is natural that the bride should desire her wedding to be as beautiful as possible. For her and her man the occasion belongs to the great hours of life.

It may become a memory, treasured for ever after, of something strong, tender, and real.

What chance does the Church, what chance do the congregation, give her? It is devastating that parson and people make such a mess of moments that should be helpful and human.

This is really important.

It is not because of any list of doctrines gone wrong or astray that the Church has lost the hearts of the people. It is because when the children turn to it in the great moments of life— of which the day when they set up a new home is assuredly one—the Church does not tell them

*"H. H. A.: Letters to a Friend." (Second series.) *G. Bles.*

in their own tongue of the wonderful works of God.

The Church has forgotten how its Lord once delighted to turn what looked like being a failure at Cana of Galilee into a social festival with a happy ending.

It is reprehensible that our weddings should lose their religious significance and become unseemly social events. We are to blame that it is so. But would not a dignified marriage service, simple and beautiful, go some way towards hushing the chatterings and irreverences?

It is sheer blindness that hinders the Church from seeing that it has no right to expect a better atmosphere to prevail at its weddings until a more real and beautiful form of service is prescribed.

WHAT IS A WELL SPENT SUNDAY?

SOME of you may remember the grim Victorian Sundays, when all the daily papers and periodicals were folded and put out of sight, when the children's toys were carefully locked in the nursery cupboard, and the only permissible entertainment was perhaps a dreary walk in Sunday clothes, and, if wet, "Peep of Day," and "no noisy games."

And I have heard of one little girl who suffered untold agony as week by week on that day of rest she had to forego the care she lavished on her dolls.

It seems so far away and fantastic as we recall such incidents in these days of hikers, and shorts, and crowded motor-coaches.

Many doubtless regret the passing of the older tradition, and join societies for the preservation of the English Sabbath, but that does not settle the problem of Sunday observance for millions who think other than they do.

The suppression of joyfulness has nothing to do with the worship of God.

Frankly, I am puzzled sometimes by the many questions which I am asked on this

[161]

subject. Is it wrong to go to the pictures or to play games on Sunday? Is there any harm in having a game of golf?

And the answer is, in my judgment, No.

There is nothing wrong in games, nor necessarily the pictures, on Sunday.

I only know what I think right for myself, and I refuse to lay down hard-and-fast rules for others to keep.

As to attending churches, that may be splendidly to the good if it be done with a desire to grow in the knowledge of God and His Will through Jesus Christ.

But, frankly, I cannot advise my friends to go on attending churches that do not, after due trial, help them to live and love better.

I am often told that you can worship God in the fields just as well as in a church. I do not for a moment deny it, but I am quite sure there are many who fancy they are worshipping Him out of doors when, as a fact, they are doing nothing of the sort.

This "blue doming" may be as weakening to character as singing sentimental hymns if it leads to no heroic effort for God or neighbour.

The Sabbath was made for man and not man for the Sabbath. It is not that certain laws are made about it and they have to be obeyed, but rather—What use am I making of it for the rest and recreation for which it was devised, recreation not for my body only, but for my soul as well?

We are in danger of forgetting that we have a soul as well as a body, and our work in life is made ineffective if we neglect the culture of the soul or mind, or whatever you prefer to call that which makes our personality.

Nowadays we are rightly careful about the culture of the body. We take good care that we get fresh air and exercise, and if five days in every week are spent in a stuffy office or workshop it is essential that we should. But our leisure is not only to be enjoyed, it has to be employed for the development of character.

Sunday is our great day. Are we employing this special time of leisure in the most serviceable way?

Are we travelling the best possible path by getting into our car on Sunday mornings and tearing off to Brighton or golf, or the pictures?

Occasionally it is of value to do so, but to keep on doing it is objectless and does not refresh or renew us. Most of us in life desire to be something other than we are. We are always hearing men say that the job they do is not what they would have chosen had they had their way.

We forget that most of us do not work more than forty or fifty hours a week. There is time for other considerations.

I make a plea, not so much for Sunday observance, as for the observance of all our leisure time.

It is only in this way that we can get a proper perspective of life as it should be lived by one who is made in the image of God.

No thing on earth created by God is in itself wrong.

It is the use to which we put that thing which makes it either a good or evil thing, and going to church may become a bad thing for me if I go, not to worship God, but to please myself or some one else, or for the sake of being respectable.

Yet, if we leave God out of our lives, we shall not achieve all we might. We shall not find those depths of feeling which will make our lives more effective.

We may become glorious animals and as fit as fiddles physically, but we have neglected the discipline which makes men of us, men worthy of doing their jobs.

Most of us need, more than we are ready to

[164]

confess, to correct our lives of drift by the discipline of an organized religion. Churches that do no violence to conscience may well be a means whereby associated mankind may seek and find eternal ideals.

Eventually each has to answer the question of Sunday observance for himself, and there is one guiding principle: Am I leading a God-centred or a self-centred life?

THERE was once a famous French lawyer, Malesherbes, who for a time was greatly loved by his countrymen.

He was the most powerful inditer of the abuses of his time, but at last he was driven out of France for his liberal and enlightened views.

At the age of seventy-four, when living in Switzerland, his old master, Louis XVI, was brought up for trial in Paris. Others refused the offer of appearing for the King, but Malesherbes said:—"I was called to the councils of my master when all the world thought it an honour to serve him, and shall I not serve him now when all the world deems it a danger?"

In defending the King, the lawyer addressed the tribunal with dignity and grace, calling Louis XVI by the old courtly title that had always been used in the proud days of Versailles.

At last his treatment of the case got on the nerves of the tribunal, and the president said to him: "From whence, sir, do you derive authority to call Louis Capet by the name that we have abolished?"

The old man looked him in the face and replied: "From my contempt for you and for my own life."

The end was foreseen, and Malesherbes followed the King to the scaffold.

A story like that makes one tingle. It is good hearing in these days.

The spectacle of a man standing by his old champion, cost what it may, when his sun has set and all the world combines to deride one whom it once delighted to honour, is sufficiently noble.

It is not a common sight, and the world has nothing much finer to show.

There are, of course, just a few who would always break a lance for their one-time benefactor, but as a rule the world forgets, and it is the new stars that have arisen in the firmament who get the applause.

Nothing seems meaner or more shocking than the average man's ingratitude for favours once received.

I am feeling this keenly at the moment, for I happened an hour since to turn up a letter from an old hero of long ago.

He died in poverty, and, since at one time his name had been on every man's lips, he had a most satisfactory funeral, amid a twenty-four-hour eruption of posthumous good will.

But if the funeral was a success, the memorial which it was proposed should be erected to commemorate him was not.

Nor do I know what happened to the trifling sum that was subscribed for the purpose.

Here is the sentence in the old man's letter that started these reflections :—

"Most of my contemporaries are dead, and the few young people who owe their success in life to me never come near me now. I am dead to them."

You will suggest that it was the old man's fault, and that he had turned into a prosy old bore, that he expected more adulation than his grown-up pupils could accord him, that he was living in very humble circumstances and a visit might have embarrassed him.

These things may be true enough, and yet they provide no excuse for those who climbed to success on the master's shoulders and then, at least seemingly, kicked him from under them.

The sacrifice of Malesherbes was not asked of them, but something very much simpler—a word of cheer and a visit now and then to an ancient and, if you will, boring old benefactor who had fallen from his high estate.

The evening of life is a tough time for the old, —to-day it is especially so,—and if not even a measure of gratitude from those they have served to the best of their ability is to be counted upon, hard indeed is their lot.

Of course, benefactors grow fractious in old age. The more fawned upon they have been in their time of success or lime-lit failure, (which also has its devotees,) the more adulation they will demand.

Of course, they grow trying in their dotage and anecdotage, but once we tried them and they bore with us, and loved us into decency or success.

It seems a despicable thing now not to defend them to the end.

It is the same with parents. They too can be difficult; they have the whip hand of us every time, if only because they got there first; but they have reason, and, (believe me,) they are right, to count on the active gratitude of those for whom they gave so much.

It is heartbreaking to think of the mothers who to-night are thanking God on their knees for children— who, to all intents and purposes, have forgotten them.

The modern contention that boys and girls owe nothing to their parents will not convince anyone save he who invented it to dull his conscience against a charge of gross and culpable ingratitude.

Many of us are guilty of this sin towards someone, and noble is he who is in the tradition of Malesherbes.

And the moral is this, that we should call round at the house that we have not visited now for many a long day, in case there may be a chance of doing something there for someone who once did a lot for us, and who is now tired, neglected, or old.

NOT so very long ago I came on this, from the writings of Rupert Brooke:

"I haven't told you much about my voyage, have I? There's not much to tell. I felt a trifle lonely before I left Liverpool; everybody seemed to have people to see them off. So I went back on shore and found a dirty little boy, who was unoccupied and said his name was William.

" 'Will you wave to me if I give you sixpence, William?' I said. 'Why, yes,' said William.

"So I gave him sixpence and went on board. When the time came he leaned over the railing on the landing stage and waved.

"Now and then he shouted indistinct messages in a shrill voice. And as we slid away the last object I saw was a small dot waving a white handkerchief, nearly white, faithfully.

"So I got my sixpenn'orth and my farewell— dear William!"

What a dreadful thing is loneliness, and how many of us need a William.*

Our teachers have told us time and again to

*"Memoirs." *Sidgwick & Jackson.*

cultivate the art of being happy alone, but there are occasions when it cannot be done, and when we suspect that even they—for all their brave words—are not able to practise what they preach.

The trouble is that there are so many forms of loneliness, and when we have beaten back one or two, on comes another ugly fellow and finds a lodgment where he has no right to be.

There are some people who say they are never lonely, but it will generally be found that these have a busy or happy background to their lives, in which case they have never really understood what aloneness means.

Those who are fortunate in this respect cannot realize what men and women suffer who really are alone.

In a sense, every thinking person must at times endure a feeling of isolation.

There is the inescapable loneliness of the great, or rather of the large mind.

A man like Napoleon must have been envied when he was in the full flood of his triumphs, but there can be no doubt that he knew, as few other men have known, what it was to be lonely. It is probably true that the dictators of the present day like Mussolini, Stalin, and Hitler must sometimes be intolerably aware that they are alone.

There are words that Bernard Shaw has put into the mouth of Joan of Arc which poignantly reveal the loneliness of a great soul.

Facing her accusers she cries: "I am alone on earth: I have always been alone . . . My father told my brother to drown me if I would not stay to mind his sheep while France was bleeding to death: France might perish if only our lambs were safe. . . .

"Do not think you can frighten me by telling me that I am alone. France is alone; and God is alone; and, what is my loneliness before the loneliness of my country and my God?

"I see now that the loneliness of God is His strength: what would He be if He listened to your jealous little counsels?

"Well, my loneliness shall be my strength too: it is better to be alone with God: His friendship will not fail me, nor His counsel, nor His love."*

What about the unspeakable loneliness of Christ?

"What, could ye not watch with Me one hour?" We lesser folk can know but little of the loneliness of the great.

Ours is of a different kind, but it hurts like fury for all that.

*"St. Joan." *Constable.*

[173]

Many of my readers will know what it means to live in lodgings, in not too easy circumstances, and to return there in the evening with no welcome awaiting, no one to talk to, no money for the pictures, no consolation at home except the gas-ring.

It must be nearly as bad to be alone in a luxury flat.

And how lonely a great city can be—the gossip of a village is better than the utter loneliness of a town that knows and cares nothing about our comings and goings.

And there is a still worse form of loneliness— and I have been meeting it lately at night in the crypt of a certain church that is always open— it is the loneliness of feeling that no one in the wide world wants you, even as a "hand" for work, let alone as a heart to love.

That is the outside misery of existence which many suffer to-day.

It's as near hell as anything in this world can be.

A few nights ago I was talking to yet another stranger, who told me that for months he had wandered around London looking for work.

And what had seared his very soul was not so much that he had not found work, but that nowhere had he found a word of kindness.

[174]

Was he exaggerating? Let us hope so, but years ago, when I lived in East London, I often accompanied men early in the morning on their dreary tramp in search of employment, and often I was shocked and surprised beyond words at the thoughtless way in which their applications would be turned down with one abrupt sentence.

An equally short one with a "Sorry, old man, and good luck," would have made all the difference in the world—the difference between the applicant going away disappointed, or going away feeling utterly alone and unwanted —suicidal.

There is not a great deal we can do to cure our neighbour's loneliness, we are hard pressed enough at times to help our own.

But at least we could be on the look-out, where we live, to see if there is anyone near by whom we could help without patronage.

And, at least, if any should approach us seeking such service as might dispel their sense of isolation we could send them away—if send them away we must—with the belief that, at any rate, one person seemed to understand and to regret being unable to help.

This is one of the elementary things that every professing Christian should take in his stride.

[175]

CENTRAL LONDON was surprised and delighted at the series of important dinner-hour cricket matches which were to be witnessed in a churchyard recently.

Surprised, for it seems impossible that on a half-acre of flagged pavement with a few straggling trees giving a handful of shade a cricket match could be played; delighted, for no one denies that Englishmen love cricket.

One saw at once a change in the faces, so often dejected, of those who sit on the wooden seats in the shelter of St. Martin-in-the-Fields because there is nothing else to do—they all became brighter and cheerful and the interest was evident.

Something was afoot, and even the windows of the local offices were at a premium.

And all this was nothing more than a cricket match which some clergy and laymen organized against local school boys and girls.

The stumps were scarcely up to standard, odd ones gathered or salvaged from some old dump or lumber room, stuck in a block of wood, all very wobbly and not one bail above the six stumps.

The bats—well! They could just be recognized as bats, good old warriors that must have made hundreds in their time.

First the two matches against the boys and the girls, which were, perhaps, the most exciting.

They certainly brought many spectators, and that made fielding somewhat difficult and life a little dangerous.

Then came the great match. Men (left hand) against Women. The score was kept by one woman, and no one to this day is really sure as to which side won.

The scoring book was not too clear on that point, and all were pleased when the best bowler among the men was taken off because he had taken a wicket.

After that incident every one in the team was allowed to bowl—it seemed fairer somehow.

Let it be recorded that in this last contest I scored a masterly captain's innings of 2.

That is what an Englishman means by playing cricket. Something to be enjoyed and laughed at and talked over, not something to wrangle over and be unpleasant about, and then write to the newspapers.

I suppose the Test matches are important, though one regrets lots about them, as well as the pavilion team of armchair experts, who should be put in inverted commas or the stocks.

As a fact, you can see the true spirit of cricket on the flagged pavement of St. Martin's more clearly than on some county grounds.

Young and old delight to watch this ancient game when it is played on village greens as it should be.

"How nice to see the dear vicar putting up the hymns," said an old woman, gazing at the scoring board at the local match.

She was there because everybody was there.

Cricket really does mean something to us in England—something more than a game to be won or lost, something inexpressible and almost religious.

It is a social and family event, an affair of good fellowship.

The cricketer is rightly a hero—alas! that I am a thing of the past in this respect, and yet I had my moment at Lord's lately, when a small boy, seeing me in an I Zingari tie, asked for my autograph, though the moment vanished when the boy, looking at my signature, said: "Excuse me, sir, what county do you play for? I've never heard of you!"

We Victorians love our memories, and the sound of bat on ball is music in our ears. What tales, what boring tales of our prowess, we have for our children.

But cricket means a lot in our character, for it is a part of our life.

A part, too, if you will permit sentiment, of old England, whether we play or watch.

And, although we prefer a green, and shady trees, and country surroundings, we shall have our contented minutes in Central London while there are folk who will play the game amid laughter and cheers, with a soft ball and an apology for a bat, without much care as to who wins.

For it means that we still have the desire to be friendly, decent, and sporting.

That silly phrase: "Playing the game," is not so foolish as the highbrows think.

A cricket match in a town churchyard can be as much a pastoral as a performance.

We shall do it again in that churchyard.

What's wrong with that?

THE following quotation from an advertisement has given me a smile:

> In London she was Mabel
>   The best of all the bunch,
> But down in his expenses
>   She was petrol, oil, and lunch.

But it also led my thoughts to the modern art of wangling, and that washed the smile away.

I don't expect you will find "wangle" in any ordinary dictionary, but, like "swank," it's a very useful word, and we all know what it means.

Indeed, most of us have done a bit of wangling in our time.

"I'll wangle that out of mother," said a small child the other day.

She meant, of course, that she wasn't sure that she could get what she wanted by straightforward tactics; she would have to use more subtle and diplomatic methods, she would have to wangle.

It is not surprising that you don't find the

word in the ordinary dictionary, for it is not a very respectable word.

There is nothing terribly wrong about it, for, as we all know, everybody does it now and then, and man's conscience can easily be squared to fit his circumstances.

But our wangling needs watching, if only because in nearly every case it is done that we may obtain some material advantage for ourselves that we know in our heart of hearts we are not entitled to.

I am sure we ought not to go on being indulgent to what a dear old lady once called "the little Piccadillyoes," for however natural or petty we may think them, they tend to undermine moral standards.

One can find many excuses for our wanglings; times are hard, official salaries are inadequate, living is infernally expensive, and although, naturally, we shouldn't dream of robbing the till or breaking into a bank, well—these small things are very different, aren't they?

And it is fatally easy to slip into the habit of doing not altogether honest acts.

Take the simple, understandable case of a youngster at his first job in the City.

He is sent on an errand to the West End. A twopenny 'bus fare, but he knows how slow the traffic can be—what is easier than to walk one way and claim fourpence for expenses from the chief clerk?

He does it, perhaps, only twice a week, but there are many weeks in the year.

Here is the beginning, and no one can say it is healthy. Little dishonesties leave their marks upon our personal character, and eventually upon our national character, of which we are so proud.

I have come to the conclusion that one cannot hold a brief for the petrol, oil, and lunch, however much Mabel—the best of all the bunch—enjoyed herself.

In the first place, it is not fair on Mabel.

It detracts from my estimation of her, for if she means anything to me other than mere enjoyment of her company, the respect in which I hold her should not let me stoop to cheat on her behalf.

It is neither fair to Mabel nor to her host that she should be entertained at someone else's expense.

If she found out she should be justly humiliated and annoyed.

A large number of otherwise perfectly honest citizens will go to any length to do a little successful wangling, to get a little something off the income-tax assessment, or travel first with a third-class ticket.

Both are dishonest, and we are well advised not to trust our fortunes or futures to those who are not above suspicion in the little things.

And it is here that we might do a little thinking. All of us still believe in honesty; our ordinary everyday lives would be unbearable if we did not.

We are so interdependent that if we did not trust our fellows to deal justly with us we should lead a miserable existence.

This wangling has got into our personal life, and, alas, it has got a firm hold on our public and commercial life, too.

I suggest that we should scotch it, for it is unrighteous, and righteousness alone exalteth a people.

Might we not stop for a moment before we contemplate our worst wangle, and see what it is that we hope to achieve by it?

Is the thing we are after so vitally important that to do without it would endanger our mortal existence?

Is the pleasure we are going to give to Mabel so intrinsically worth while that we would steal in order to obtain it?

[183]

For that is exactly what we are doing.

My plea is that we should try, say for one week, to see if we can get along without wangling.

If I were asked to give a definition of the word "wangle" for a slang dictionary, here it is:—

WANGLE, v. *i.v.t.* (whatever that may mean to lexicographers): To take advantage of, to cheat without appearing dishonest, to make life easy for myself without expenditure of effort on my part. (*See* Dirty Work.)

THE late Lord Curzon used to tell a charming story against himself.

When he was a young man a French governess asked him the meaning of the word "bounder," which, she said, someone had applied to him.

"A bounder, my dear young lady," explained Lord Curzon, "is one who advances by leaps and bounds."

I have just had no end of a row with such a one, and, though the air is still blue as a result, I have no regrets.

My opponent—an able man—has become an assured success. He has advanced rapidly, too rapidly, by leaps and bounds, and it has not done him much good.

He is neither as likeable nor as effective as he was.

He now enjoys hearing the voices of little people saying what a great man he is, and he has no use for those who will not join in the chorus.

The poor fellow has actually reached the stage of rebuking old friends who speak of him by the nickname that distinguished him at school. It wasn't Biffin, but it was a name of that kind.

I fear it is rather a desperate case.

This may sound carping and nasty, but I am going to let it stand, for the type I am up against is very common and terribly oppressive. And Biffin—let us call him that—has gone particularly mouldy.

He not only boasts of what he has already done in public life and what he proposes to do in the near future, but he will drag in the fact that socially he is also a howling success.

He calls famous and good-looking women by their Christian names and hints that they confide in him.

He is apparently invited everywhere to meet "all the best people," and twice he told me that later that day he would attend the afternoon party at the Great House.

It was nauseating and silly stuff, and when I heard this last item of news for the second time I could stand it all no longer. I uttered one word, but it sufficed.

I said: "Swank." Then Biffin and I were at it hammer and tongs for thirty minutes.

Poor Biffin, he reminds me of the brilliant and conceited young man of whom Mr. Gladstone remarked : "There goes a young man with a great future behind him."

This is not written down in malice towards Biffin, who no doubt is a good enough fellow in his way, like the rest of us. It is rather a warning for those—of whom there are a surprising number—who are travelling in the same disastrous direction.

Nothing is more disappointing than to watch someone with real ability beginning to throw his weight about the moment he gets into the saddle.

I have known more men morally destroyed by getting a rise than by remaining year in and year out where they were.

I have watched quite admirable workmen becoming impossible foremen, estimable vicars becoming intolerable bishops, and budding politicians becoming pompous administrators.

It was swank that was doing them in and ruining careers that might have been genuinely serviceable.

Possibly now and then a man or a woman may arise big enough to throw his or her weight about and get away with it, but as a general rule the successful man will have nothing more to contribute if he shed his original simplicity.

"I can't speak to my old friend any more,"

said a man to me last week. "You see, he's
Gawd Almighty now."

There are several antidotes for Biffinism.

An excellent one is to remember the advice
that the painter, William Orpen, once gave. He
said that everyone should be taught to con-
jugate this verb:—

> I am a joke,
> Thou art a joke,
> He is a joke,
> We are jokes,
> Ye are jokes,
> They are jokes.

If those of us who are inclined to swank
would have a good laugh, especially at ourselves, it would help quite a lot.

But we who profess Christianity must remember besides that the Founder of our religion
made claim to two virtues alone—meekness and
lowliness.

They were not accounted virtues in His time,
nor are they highly thought of to-day, but now,
as then, the ideal service is performed only by
those who refrain from bombinating, who do
not throw their weight about, who retain their
simplicity and do not swank.

The World which for its
   Babels needs a scourge,
And for its wilds a husbandman,
   acclaims
The Crucified that came of Nazareth.

DURING those days which lead up to
Eastertide the Christian Church rehearses
yet again the ancient tragedy that culminated
in the Crucifixion of Jesus Christ.

It will do so the more compellingly if it
refrains from over-much explanation, comment-
ary, and marginal notes, allowing the sacred
narrative to speak for itself.

Nothing is more significant in the Gospels
than the way in which the death of Christ is
recorded. Where we look for eulogy, flattery,
and sympathy, we do not find them.

There is little of the adjective in the story, no
heroics, no pious "Ohs and Ahs," no great
passages of explanation or commendation, and
no treatise on the Atonement.

There is no abuse of Herod or Pilate, no

censure of those who played their several parts on the day of Crucifixion.

It seems as if the writers were wholly unanxious to write themselves into the narrative.

They had something of tremendous import to tell, and there was no need of embellishment: the plain story was enough and more than enough. That story is sublime in its simplicity, a perfect work of art, a triumph of restraint: it suffers less from the eternal inadequacy of human intelligence than any story that is known to man.

It guarantees its own reliability, but more—it teaches (I think) how the Christ may be revealed to men.

So many more hungry people would know Him as Lord and Saviour if only we had the faith to say: "Behold the Man."

Did we but suffer the deathless words of our Lord from the Cross to be heard just as they were spoken and not rush men on at once at our own pace to our own conclusions—however true they be—we should be wiser ambassadors.

At Calvary, Jesus can make His own way better than we can make way for Him. There He is and says what all men, who have not forsworn their values and have cleared a space

[190]

in their lives for the spiritual, can recognize as being of God.

The Seven Words from the Cross, unaccompanied by a preacher's eloquence and exhortation, will disturb the heart and linger more hauntingly and longer on the conscience than any official or pontifical utterance.

That is the way of every voice that cries truth in the wilderness, and truth is ultimate, supreme, and final in the dying words of Jesus Christ.

Our Lord was never more in control of the human conscience, never more at home in the human heart or in the world than when He withdrew to the Cross.

From there He speaks the wisdom and compassion which are not of this world, but which are too plain for the misunderstanding of any who know the immutable difference between right and wrong.

We religious people need not sentimentalize the Cross nor spin our elaborate theories about it on Good Friday, lest in trying to explain we explain our Lord away.

When we entomb Christ in contentious words He has a way of going on ahead where the simple and straightforward may not find Him. Best let Him speak for Himself, in His own words, for His speech is the dialect of every human heart that knows its sin and sorrow.

Jesus is His own credential, and it is lack of faith, and not belief in Him, when we insist upon making Him say less or more than He did.

He remains the heart and soul of the Christian movement, still—if we would but see—controlling every situation, still capturing men, even sometimes against their will.

He is never so superbly in control as when He is reigning from the tree on which He died for those who would or could not understand His wisdom.

It is the deepest instinct in the heart of man that where sacrificial love is, there God is also.

There is one spirit, as it has been said, whose divinity no man can deny, and that is the undaunted spirit that keeps on loving, even in the abyss, when love goes unrewarded.

Even the Roman centurion cries "The Son of God", when a soul can bear the contumely and pain of crucifixion and make the prayer from the Cross that can still cause us to tingle: "Father forgive them for they know not what they do."

We know as we stand at Calvary that man, too, will only save his life and world by losing

[192]

both, by daily dying on his lesser Calvary in the spirit of the just man made perfect through suffering.

Death has no dominion here. The way has been blazed for us. "Death thou shalt die."

Christ haunts us, and never so violently, so persuasively and yet so fearfully, as when we attend to the unedited gospel of His Cross.

"I, if I be lifted up, will draw all men unto Me."

That is the beginning, but there is much to follow whereof we shall know if we can but persevere.

LAST year, I rather expected a letter from one of my less friendly critics to remind me that Easter coincided most appropriately (in his judgment) with All Fools' Day. It came.

Well, well, my anonymous correspondent is welcome to his little joke, if joke it be and joke he must, but I hope he will permit me to say that the Resurrection of Jesus Christ—be it true or false—is scarcely a subject for levity.

The Eternal Hope touches very deep and tender places in the human heart, and to dismiss it with a gibe is totally unworthy. The question of immortality is not one which has been invented by pedants and priests for puzzlement or profit.

It is not an abstract proposition; it has arisen and it abides in the soul of man as he looks out upon the mystery of his being.

And ah, to know not, while with friends
    I sit,
  And while the purple joy is passed about,
Whether 'tis ampler day divinelier lit
  Or homeless night without;

And whether, stepping forth, my soul shall see
  New prospects, or fall sheer—a blinded
    thing!
There is, O grave, thy hourly victory,
  And there, O death, thy sting.

If the Christian hope of resurrection—which
is more than mere survival—be true, it is too
grandly true to be joked about; if false, it is too
greatly false, too tragically false, for humour.

If Christ be not risen, then vain indeed is the
belief of millions; they have lived and loved and
lost; that is not funny.

If our subject demands intellectual honesty,
as it certainly does, it also requires to be ap-
proached with reverence.

My correspondent tells me at length that he
is totally uninterested now in what happens
when this life is over. But, like me, he too has a
rendezvous with death, and he will probably
find then that the subject is of considerable
moment—indeed, the last interest that he will
have.

The rest of the long letter is a personal
attack on me for declaring that the irreligious
will be damned eternally.

I can be criticized on many counts, but not
on that particular one, for I have never said or

thought any such thing, though I have suspected there must be a hell here or hereafter when I have seen a child or a dog tortured and have been debarred by conscience from torturing the torturer.

Actually I believe that while none of us are quite good enough for Heaven, none of us are quite bad enough for hell, and my deepest conviction is that *ultimately* not one of God's children will be lost.

Perhaps the wisest word on this matter has recently been written by a leading Christian philosopher. After quoting the opinion of another writer that "if there are really diabolical men, no doubt their destiny is perdition, but I should hope that such men are very few" —Professor Taylor adds: "I should like myself to hope that there are none such, but there is just one man of the many whom I have known, about whom I feel that it is salutary not to be over sanguine, myself."

Let me testify to what I believe, though I cannot hope to influence my friend and those who think with him.

There are times, it seems to me, when faith must reign supreme, into which reason can only dare to penetrate as a wondering child, clutching at Faith's hand and asking for guidance and illumination.

One thing only holds, then—passionate, instinctive, irrational (if you will) belief in the goodness of God as seen in the streets of Galilee, on the Cross of Calvary, and on Easter Day when the Conqueror came striding down the garden early in the morning.

Turn up that lovely chapter—the twentieth— in St. John's Gospel and read about it.

There is much, very much, that makes it hard to believe that God is love, but it is harder still to believe that all is an accident. A great deal is hidden from our sight in mystery.

> Yet, in the maddening maze of things,
> And tossed by storm and flood,
> To one fixed trust my spirit clings,
> I know that God is good.

We must ask for truth and not for a fairy tale. There is merit as well as blame in the doubt that says: "Except I see and touch I will not believe."

But when all is said and argued, the fact remains that "we do not believe in a life hereafter because we have proved it, but we for ever try to prove it because we believe it." "The Churches," writes Dr. Carnegie Simpson—"or at least their theologies—overload faith."

It is not necessary to believe much if only we

can believe well; and even a Christian if he be a good believer about the essential things can afford to be a good agnostic about the rest.

I have thus nothing to offer to those who raise curious speculations about a further life; nor am I disposed to discuss with those who peer through the keyhole of the door to another world and bring dubious reports of trivial happenings there.

In the supreme issue of human destiny, when the overpowering ebb is sweeping someone dear to us, or shall sweep us, far out into the dark deep, it is enough if we can say with the Prince of Believers, who is also the surety of our souls: "Father, into *Thy* hands."

The first day of April is a grand day for Easter Day, and those who can accept all that April means need not find the Resurrection incredible. Our dear Lord *has* harrowed hell. Death, thou shalt die.

And if it be said, as it well may be, that I have proved nothing, I can only answer: "No, alas, I have not. I cannot. I can only confess my faith."

I SUPPOSE this heading may sound a bit ridiculous, but it need not.

Christianity presupposes a certain type of man and woman—a certain kind of father, mother, brother, sister, friend and neighbour; a certain kind of employer, employee—the sort that in every circumstance can be counted upon to act unconsciously like a gentle-man or a gentle-woman.

Why should not Christianity, which is nothing if not relevant, presuppose a certain kind of shopper?

It is said that there are a million or so Christians in London alone, but I'll be bothered if you could find a lot of them in the shops just now, and I doubt if those who forward the goods know the addresses of many!

One is tempted to suspect that Christians have given up Christmas shopping, which is highly ridiculous.

I saw a lady buying a Father Christmas the other day, and if I had been that Father Christmas I should not only have refused to return home with her, but I should have given her particular chimney-pot a miss on Christmas Eve, and added her present to the parcel due for the poor girl who had been obliged to serve her.

Perhaps the purchaser was not a Christian; we will hope not for the credit of her Church.

All this is no plea for shoppers who cannot distinguish glitter from gold, nor for an aggressive friendliness for which the young lady on the other side of the counter may have neither time nor use, but only that when Christians go shopping they should shop like Christians, like gentle-folk.

Here are a few memos:—

(1) Those who are serving are probably pretty tired; standing all day is very hard work.

(2) They have troubles like us, probably, and less time and money for their Christmas shopping.

(3) Perhaps after the Christmas rush they will be out of work again.

(4) Need people be courteous to us unless we are courteous to them? Try being civil to strangers daily from nine to six and then over-time.

(5) Don't blame assistants for what their

shops do not stock or stock inadequately—it is not their fault.

(6) Don't get every single box off the shelf for the fun of seeing what is there and buying it elsewhere.

(7) Don't thumb everything you don't buy. Scotland Yard may want our finger-prints, but they are not wanted elsewhere.

(8) Even shop assistants have only two eyes, two hands and two legs. A pity, but there it is.

(9) Say "Thank you."

I should count it a great privilege to shake the hand of the manager of any store who, after instructing his staff, pasted those nine memos on his shop windows.

Of course, there are some aggravating shop assistants; like medicine, they need shaking regularly before they do any good; some, too, who are less civil to us than we to them, but the wonder is that, seeing what they have to put up with, the large majority are so courteous and long suffering.

The art of shopping like a Christian, like gentle-folk, consists in preparing ourselves on the way to the shop to meet a human being, a living soul, a brother or a sister behind the counter.

Why not?

I wonder if my readers know the prayer called St. Patrick's Breast Plate? It begins:—

May the strength of God pilot us

And ends:—
May Christ be with us. Christ before us. Christ in us. Christ over us.

The world could do with a few more Christian shoppers just now.

CHRISTMAS EVE finds us a long way from the Inn at Bethlehem. We should like to be there, but nowadays we only talk prose; there is little poetry left within us, you can hear few strings and much wind in the sounds we make.

It was not always so. There was a time when, for us, angels and fairies were very real. In those far-off days undoubtedly, too, there were shepherds and wise men and kings about on Christmas Eve, and there was even an angelic choir chanting on the hills of Bethlehem.

How incredibly foolish, but it was very long ago, and we were young and romantic.

Now, of course, we are sophisticated and know better. We are not seeing visions any more, and as for that angelic choir, if it exists at all, it cannot be heard down our way, in Belgravia, Bermondsey or wherever we live.

It is hard for us to travel with good heart towards Christmas, for our road is dark and there is no star now to guide us. We cannot be hopeful or happy to order, or burst into singing because the vicar announces a Christmas hymn.

Romance has had a terrible doing in recent

years; it seems to have been battered out of recognition and almost expelled off the face of the earth. Look wistfully where we may, we cannot find it, and without it we may not start for Bethlehem. We have lost the way.

And yet if we did but know it, it is just here that God comes in with His greatest device of love. Call Him Hound of Heaven or Child of Bethlehem, He will not let His children go.

On the Cross or in the cradle He will be alongside suffering, struggling humanity. He will insert Himself into the very path down which we travel in hope or despair, for He is not only the Way, but on the way.

Was there ever a Device of Love more compelling than the Child of Bethlehem?

> They all were looking for a king,
>   To slay their foes and set them high;
> Thou cam'st a little baby thing
>   That made a woman cry.

"What are you going to do about Christmas?" said a wife to her husband. "Nothing," said he, "it is bound to come." So it is—thank God. Glory to God in the highest, and on earth peace, good will towards men. Christmas is on the way—it is bound to come. It will get us whether we feel like it or not.

Yield to it, gladly, wistfully or reluctantly, but yield we must. Christmas Day is inevitable. That is its wonder and our hope. Give in to it as freely as you can. Make, not the best, but the most, of it.

For it means that for twenty-four brief hours we really *shall* have peace and good will among men; for twenty-four hours in our winter's darkness the spell of the Kingdom of God will be actually upon us and our world.

We shall be decenter, more likeable, more understanding people; beside one another, and not beside ourselves any longer, and for one whole day.

Little enough, but better than we, with the wisdom of this world, can achieve. If only the Christmas truce could be carried over into the days that lie ahead. If only we would go with the Man to Jerusalem, and not merely croon to the Child at Bethlehem.

"Hail to the little Lord at Christmas," but need we add "and farewell?"

Be glad and happy if you may to-morrow, my friends (forgive my Christmas Eve presumption). I covet every kind of good thing for you, and over and above all the heavenly and homely sounds of Christmas, one especial noise—"a master noise . . . the noise of great

[205]

fat cheques being ripped violently from their moorings and presented unawares to poor men.

> Match me such marvel, whether East
>   or West,
> So full of blooming ecstasy and zest.*"

A happy Christmas!

*D. Wyndham Lewis.

"IT'S not much fun," said a grumpy friend, "for a fellow who wants to sleep on in the morning to hear you bawling in the bathroom about that old blighter Wenceslas."

I answered him pretty sharply. I said that, leaving aside the question as to whether I bawled or sang, it was the Christmas spirit, and I was getting him into form without charging him anything. I said he ought to like it.

I also said that if I heard one word more of this most unseasonable complaining he'd get "Good Christian men rejoice!" on the morrow, and an hour earlier, too.

Actually, I was just a little sorry for my friend —an owl, and not a lark—but I am not to be browbeaten around Christmas.

The pessimists have had a good innings and we really need not apologize for being cheerful just now, provided, in the presence of those who suffer, that we lend a hand and are not clumsily exuberant; provided also that our merriment is spontaneous, and not worked up.

I once knew a clergyman who gave me the impression one Christmas morning that he was hard at work loving his "people," and prepared to make merry with them officially at all costs from 9 a.m. to 12.45 p.m. precisely.

It was his duty, and he would see it through. A painful sight.

I am not advocating an official manifestation of the Christmas spirit, not even carols in the bathroom unless (as in my own case) you cannot help it; but only that those able to receive the Gospel story should rejoice in it and in their own (possibly quiet) way let it be seen that Christianity can indeed encourage the high spirits of the soul.

In so far as in us lies we will travel happily as well as hopefully towards Christmas.

We will move out gladly towards Bethlehem, proud and fortunate in our belief that the light that is above, within and from the Inn is the Light of the World—both its safety and its danger.

I have an anthology which a friend compiled for me. Like most beautiful things that are new, it is not yet complete.

Under the dark days and dates of December there are blank pages, but this week the Unfinished Anthology begins to sing again in this sort of way:—

[208]

I saw a stable, low and very bare,
A little Child in a manger,
The oxen knew Him, had Him in their
   care.
To men He was a stranger.
The safety of the world was lying there
And the world's danger.*

Around Christmas human speech breaks down. We have to call in poetry, carols, music, pictures, pageantry and Christmas trees to express the glory and wonder of the Child of Bethlehem—our safety and our danger, as well as our joy.

I write this early in the morning. I have just come from the bathroom, where I sang "Good Christian men rejoice!"

*Mary Coleridge's Poems. *Elkin Mathews* & *Marrot.*

THE mortality among New Year resolutions is phenomenal.

Even January 1st has many a casualty. I hope it does not reveal a lack of humour to submit that the breaking of good resolutions a few hours or days after they have been made is not as humorous as we sometimes suppose.

There are some jokes that are good all through, and others—like laughing at a drunkard—that may look amusing on the surface, but are not really funny at all.

Among the latter, I suggest the inclusion of those that depend for their point on our inability to keep our promises to God and man. There is no humour here, only a tragedy.

It is the crime that curses us that the good that we would, we do not; while the evil that we would not, that we do.

Of course, we do not laugh when we ourselves are the victims of a broken pledge; but when the resolution of a friend crashes, then the merriment begins.

And if the crash involves his descent once more to our level, to become again what we call "a good sport," how jolly for us and our crowd!

The leader of the Group Movement is very fond of saying that "the banana that leaves the bunch gets skinned," but I know quite a few bananas who are likely to lose a great deal more than their skins unless they leave their particular bunch. And pretty quick, too.

The ugliest laughter in the world—laughter that has hell in it—is that which comes from gross men as they welcome the poor prodigal returning to their wallow, with his broken resolution trailing behind.

It is no occasion for hilarity. Were we to proclaim our bad resolution and then go to it, there might at least be time for the police to step in, but this business of declaring what fine fellows we are about to become and then standing still is the very devil. Had we then better refrain from all New Year resolutions of amendment since their record is so chequered?

What is the good of these ineffective promises to God and man?

They are born in a moment of emotion; born on a cold December night into surroundings neither welcoming nor congenial.

They must live with us and meet our friends, be nourished there or die.

What chance have they? Almost none, indeed, until we recognize that no resolution, however noble, can live unless it falls naturally into its surroundings and is carried along and nourished there. As well expect a hot-house plant to thrive in the refrigerator as a new-born resolution in a life into which it does not fit.

It can grow and live and last only when it is made welcome and at home. A good man can absorb any amount of good resolutions without being puffed up. A selfish man may take them in for a moment, but he will not keep them down. They will not stay his way.

It is new life rather than new resolutions that we need. For our encouragement we may remember that Christianity, grimly serious about man's unaided efforts, is grandly optimistic about what he may become under the hand of Him whose gospel is not good advice but good news, and Who gives to those who dare to ask it of Him "the power to become." These can take good resolutions in their stride.

Christian, seek not yet repose.